I0786046

"Advertising has us chasing cars and clothes, working jobs we hate so we can buy shit we don't need. We are the middle children of the history man, no purpose or place, we have no Great war, no Great depression, our great war is a spiritual war, our great depression is our lives. We've all been raised on television to believe that one day we'd all be millionaires, and movie gods, and rock stars. But we won't. And we're slowly learning that fact. And we are very, very pissed off"

—Tyler Durden, ("Fight Club" film.)

THE ABYSS OF THE SELF.
(How to survive deepest nihilism?)

By Don Nieve.

Published by Don Nieve

CONTENTS

Here I am, trying to write you a letter. An extensive letter. A summary of all this time. From all these experiences. I don't know who you are. I don't know where the story of your life, or of your death, will have gone. I don't know if you've come out of the abyss, or if you'll be fully adapted to it. Maybe what I'm proposing now, will be definitive for you. Or maybe it's just an episode, in this sea of events, that constitutes the very existence.

Don't laugh at me, or judge me harshly. My intention is to try to guide you, to support you. Or at least, keep you company in moments of unbearable pain.

I am now 31 years old, it is September, Monday, the 12th of 2011. This is addressed to you, or rather to myself. What difference does it make? When I read this again, if I do, I'll be a different person. Each new day, each new or recurring thought that passes through you, changes you, makes you another. It shapes you, defines you, deforms you.

The water that flows through a river is not the same, even if it doesn't look like it. In this way, our being, the entity that defines us and we call "I", could be compared to the water of the river. And our body, in its course. So, on a more elementary material level, our most immediate neural connections, our energy, that's what we would be.

And the memories? Do they not influence us in a constant, integrated, invariant way, ours? Are they not permanently coded, capable of being recalled at will? How can we be tied to a nervous immediacy, which forms an elusive, ambiguous present, on horseback from the past and the future, timeless?

The truth is, for this virtual database of information to exist, a continuous flow of energy is necessary. Energy generated chemically, translating perceptive, external and own signals. Shaping our thoughts, joy, nightmares, passions, and that which we call heart. This is the root of our spirit ultimately.

Our whole construction of the 'I' is fictitious. It is adaptive to have an identity, but it is an illusion. A brilliant chimera designed and implemented by the different components of our nervous system. If these structures function properly, the connection with this reality will be intense. If there is a disorder, the identity is conflictive, and the connection with this reality is weightless.

Anyway, I'm not going to try to be very scientific, because I'm not an outright defender of rationality, and the limitations of a speech of this kind. Besides, I'm very lazy when it comes to protocols. I get desperate and bored with terrible ease.

I'm bold, but I'm not arrogant or presumptuous. I possess the courage of a dog that doesn't feel at home. Which may be expendable. That he has nothing to protect, nothing to lose, nothing to fervently desire, or to which he is attached. Like I was in one movie, and I should be in another, but I don't know which one. I feel like I'm in an abyss.

It is curious how the sensation of falling resembles the dizzying feeling of the ascent. It is possible that he is a romantic, or a depressive subject, according to psychology manuals.

I only know that I am surrounded by darkness, infinite emptiness, the absence of everything, even fear. Shortness of breath, near-sensory isolation. And yet, for the moment, I've never felt better, freer.

I have learned to forgive myself, to love myself, to enjoy that valley of shadows, which has always been there. It doesn't seem like a one-off thing, as I've been in this situation for many years, and I've been struggling all my life to stop the fall.

That's why as a firewall, either because someone reads this, or because I have risen to the surface of existence, I'm going to define it in stages. With previous indicators of not continuing. Because, while it may only make you laugh, it may also hurt your mind.

I don't know if I would have achieved this result, if all my humble goals had been met, or if I had been born in another era, if I was a bird, the wind, or a star... I may be heading for it sooner or later. Maybe it's something that has to happen to everyone, even if it's only at the moment of their elderly age, or their imminent and conscious death...

1. Base camp.

The camp is, metaphorically, the place where we all (or almost all) grow up. It is made up of society and its rules.

A society separated from the ecosystem, from the world, from the reality of the universe. Fenced by an idea:

Life and death are clearly distinguishable, and even conflicting, concepts.

The earth, as a planet, framed in a stable, linear and limited universe. An idea of right and wrong.

The feeling that we are special, in the presence of an indefinable being. It is clearly protective and kind, angry, but fair; a parent who won't leave us, if we do the right thing.

The belief that all the terrible things that happen to other people are because they deserve it. In the case of believing that his pain, or his fatal fate, is bad luck, we know in our hearts that he will not touch us. Because we're special. Because that always happens to others. Because we have to have faith, hope. We must hope that things, if they can be resolved, will work out on their own, by means of more or less religious prayers. And because this optimism will shield us from all evil.

Ours is a very fair society in which each one of us does our part in what we call security and well-being. If a person sets his mind to it, and is tenacious, he can achieve whatever he wants. Whether working or studying, the doors of the various systems are open. Most of us are educated, and we try to help each other, wanting the best for our neighbor.

The existence of values, of a conscience, of an honour. The feeling of loving something, or someone. The inner commitment to follow or support this person, no matter what happens. All this, since the beginning of humanity, has been more or less guided by religion. From the most remote or millennial tribes, come concepts that have common denominators: a creation made by God or gods and a faith submissive to them. That is, they take the blame for the consequences of living, thanks to a concept that has always fascinated, frightened, and disoriented man, almost as much or more than death: ***freedom.***

The concept of freedom, for me, is simply to be a slave to oneself. And if you feel close to a god, or comparable love, you better be a slave to them.

The alternative to not feeling that love and protection is independence, individuality, loneliness.

To be free and to serve yourself is mainly necessary one thing: to know who you are.

Science, curiosity, unraveling the truth.... Science seeks to kill God. If you are able to reconcile the idea of a creative and paternal entity with science, you better stay there, and do not want to leave the camp. Outside, only the shadows await, and the cold of the infinite emptiness.

If you believe in evolution, following in its footsteps, inevitably leads you to the nothing.

We are descended from the monkey, from life. Life, from the rational point of view, inevitably descends from matter. And this one, in turn, comes from the nothing.

So, nothingness can be that generating entity that we call God. But this God is neither protective nor just. He's not even someone to watch over our actions. He is only an indifferent God. He has no emotions. He is a cold and distant God, who cares nothing about what he does or what happens to his supposed son.

And I say so-called son, because for this generating system, we are probably just a consequence of his being. A result of the act of drinking, such as burping. Or flatulence, from eating.... The consequence of copulation, which can be children or venereal diseases. In short, we are probably only the reaction to the act of being, of the essence of the universe, of God. This way, we are not his favorite children. We are not his most precious creation. *We're probably just a subproduct, rubbish.*

By this I do not mean that we are negative, or that God hates us. I simply intend to say that we are merely an epiphenomenon of a movement that escapes our understanding: *the continuous movement of energy.*

The constant transformation, beyond the big bang, beyond the death of the universe.

So your life, framed in this existential context, finds this truth. One of many truths, right. But undoubtedly, the most likely and accurate.

How can the spirit survive with this burden? How can we carry on day by day, when today's religion, that of pleasure, of consumption, does not fill us up? How then can you give meaning to your life? If you are a person of the deep, of those who need a reason, a foundation, however small this value may be, and you do not find it, you are wrecked. Welcome to nihilism.

Most things in our lives are based on a lot of lies. You remember, since I was a kid, it just didn't feel right. And when I say this, I mean all the constructions that make up existence; society, the fragile balance of the planet, our lives. And why not, our self.

Lies, yes. It is like creating a cloud of cotton inside the most inhospitable forest, and then filling that cloud of darkness in turn. Create rules and regulations so that the naive, the unwary, the weak, can easily fall and be food for the superior predators. Many different species masked in the ability to twist, to bend, artistically, thanks to the instrument of intellect and imagination.

Rationality is used as a tool.

For those who instrumentalize it, do not center the essence of their being on it. They center it in their hearts. With the same kind of procedure and behavior of the beings with heart from outside the camp: like animals.

And it's just that thinking with your heart, it's too much. It is addictive; so addictive that many of them even kill, or hurt themselves, just for the pleasure of it.

I do not mean, by the term rationality, high speeches like Kant's. It would be more like the kind of reason Goleman proposes: a minimum of emotional intelligence. The ability to add one plus one, with peace of mind, after a light meditation and a certain judgment at the time of its execution. Any simple, happy, adapted person can do this. No high IQ is required.

What happens is that it is very difficult to talk a little bit with yourself, to know yourself, to order the house of thoughts that is your mind, your spirit. And I'm not surprised. The sophisticated person of today finds it so complex, boring, useless. After all, they are too busy receiving and sending empty information in the incredible social networking world of cyberspace. Damn, but they even have a hard time walking.

But the world, our society, far from teaching us how to handle our feelings, seems to have taught us the refined art of defecating in a box, putting fragrances and perfumes in it, closing it, adorning it with a bow, and selling your excrement at the price of gold. Everyone exchanging these precious gifts. From my point of view, fascinating.

2. Outside the camp.

It's an interesting exercise, going outside of what you know, and re-evaluating everything from a new perspective. With this ***analogy of an elephant's vision,*** it is understood quite well:

Most people, (fortunately for them, if they are adapted), are looking at an elephant's buttocks. The truth is that they see nothing else, because they are simply too close.

Some are able to move, to leave their position, their point of view. Even if they move, they're still close. For these, it is possible to see the elephant in its total fullness. The beast is shown to them parcelled, fragmented, like the pieces of a puzzle. Even so, it is very difficult for them to integrate it mentally, in an objective way, into a Gestalt totality. This is because their field of vision is limited. They cannot cover the whole of the animal, as they are not far enough apart. And that's because you have to step back, get out of the system, out of yourself, in order to be an observer of the whole scene. Walk away...

The point of view, of those who can move in the short distance, would be something like when in the Middle Ages, they made those maps that were far from the real proportions. They had traveled all the way across the continent. And even if they had more or less precise instruments, they seemed to lack that point of reference that offers them the possibility of simply seeing, simply, of perceiving the real dimension of the world from outer space.

When you separate yourself from the elephant, and stop having your head stuck up his butt, you see the pachyderm in its entire splendor.

The funny thing, the problem, the fun, the dizzying and disturbing thing is that you see yourself, along with others, surrounded by them. Very close to the elephant.

"How strange" you say to yourself. "Who is this guy? Could it be me? But how can I be, if I'm here? Who am I then? How can I be both at once if I see their separate and clearly distinguishable component elements?"

Not only is it hard to do this exercise, but it is also dangerous. It's funny at first. You can easily return and tell those around you what you have seen as curious things. They watch you, with that look that shows affectionate distrust. They see a visionary, a madman, a weird guy. Nice, friendly, eccentric, funny, but weird. You are not openly misjudged, although you can notice the distance of caution implicit in their behavior towards you.

Most of all, it shows, because even with the simplest or most sophisticated explanation of your point of view, in your moments of profound

seriousness, you are not taken seriously at all.
You're a separate case. Your judgment, the
exposure of your thoughts, your feelings, is always
a joke.

*But if you start to get curious, little by little, the
return will be more expensive. Adaptation to your
physical, social, or self environment will be more
painful. Every time you go out, you change. You are
suffocated by the pain of tedium and boredom
produced by moral, social, mental, emotional,
absurd, hypocritical rules. You're getting tired of the
comedian role you're forced to play. You don't have
the strength left to endure the trivial and
unconnected multitasking that shapes your life. You
hold on, until you have the courage, or you have no
choice but to look straight ahead, without veils.*

You look around. Everything's the same, nothing's
changed. What happens is that now you see
everything more clearly, but it is intense,
overflowing, uncontrollable, it hurts. And as if
these incursions were a drug, you need more and
more, until you are definitely lost in existential
space.

As if an astronaut were going out into space by
himself, and observing the Earth. Spit from the
Earth by an irresistible, inexplicable,
uncontrollable force. No landmarks, no supports,
no knowing if you'll be able to come back. Feeling
the terrifying emptiness and darkness that opens
up behind you. Listening to your own breathing,

and your heartbeat. Knowing in this way that you are alive, or that you at least fit that definition. Bitter is the return to earth, equally terrible to be lost.

To leave the camp is to flirt with the darkness, to dance with death, and to return victorious, having taken away some virtue from him. It's the concept of the hero, a visionary, a moron with ideas for change.

Today I write this, but remember what you wrote when you were 16, about what it was like to study all things from the point of view of wholeness:

*"**What is philosophizing?** To philosophize is to go out of oneself, out of one's country, out of the world, into infinity, and thanks to his help, to lift oneself up in the arms of God, judging everything as if you were simultaneously a prisoner, a jury, a witness, and a judge" (Now I would add: and an executioner). Only in this way is it possible to understand what matters most in life.*

Of all the regions of the universe, I ended up in the solar system. And here, I was lucky enough to get to earth; a planet full of life and curious things. I flew over the world, and fell into a first world country, Spain. It coincided, that even though my father didn't want to go out that night, he met my mother. Love arose. And then, my spirit or energy, was deposited in that conception. I was born healthy, and surrounded by affection. So why should my spirit be so troubled by the idea of the most important thing?

The most important thing in life is life itself.

Life is a gift that has been given to us, with the purpose of making us enjoy it, to squeeze it to the maximum. It is the most precious asset in the universe, the most complex and difficult to reach. There must be an innumerable set of variables, so specific, that to waste or complain about such a great gift is a sin against God and rationality. No matter what kind of life you have to live. All are a gift, even if you live the life of a dog, an insect, or a plant."

It is evident that this positive perspective clashes with the negative or neutral feeling produced by the previous one: the vision that we are only a failure of the system, an error, something that is left over.

The good thing about an indifferent God is that he gives you the choice of both senses, for a path to which everything will stop. Let everyone choose the one they can, or like.

In my case, they alternate. At the same time, but separate. The same way you can have chocolate and vanilla ice cream. The taste goes together, but separately. So that you can distinguish chocolate on one side and vanilla on the other. I guess the taste, after mixing the two flavors before freezing, would be different. What would it be called? Vanichoco? Like coffee with milk....

But, what the hell! That's how your head works sometimes. Recurrent with thoughts, until it becomes almost obsessive, free of order of priority, timeless. Jumping from memories as vivid as if they were present, to future thoughts as real as memories. All this going through a strange present, alien to me, to my desires, to my control. So don't take my constant digressions into account. Or rather, my damn mess. That's the way life is. It's better not to use language to make up for the obvious.

In any case, this is how I started my journey through the camp. Full of hope and learning well, quickly, with the Greek classics, the metaphysical interpretation through religion, of Dante, Calderon and his life as a dream, the adventures of Tenorio, as if he were a James Bond of another time, Don Quixote, Shakespeare .... and so many other good teachers, who showed you a way, which seemed to lead to the answer of almost all your questions.

These hopes were well-founded; because it seemed that throughout history, there seemed to be a pattern in all human hearts. It was as if they were always the same actors, with slight changes in their role, playing their part, in the tragicomic film of life. A small point, which made it impossible to solve the puzzle, is what you wrote observing a black and white comic book (you need the white of the paper, and the black of the ink to see the drawing):

"Is humanity defined by its side of light? Is humanity defined by its dark side? Or is it rather that the human being defines himself, is he what he is, by his contrast?"

<u>**To be or to be temporarily.**</u>

This seems like a concept, which I think synthesizes everything I learned from the Greek philosophers. Aside from a lot of messes and paradoxes, everyone tries to find out what the essence of things is, of ourselves. They look for the way this essence interacts.

In short, the essence is the being: that which does not change and remains unchanged. The being, our "I", should be able to define our spirit, our supposed soul.

In our language, we are already misleading and deluding ourselves by referring to phrases such as:

"I am young", "I am president", "I am a mother", "I am a living being"... etc. The meaning changes considerably if we change being, to being temporarily, which is how it should be. To be temporarily, refers to qualities considered as transitory, and to be refers to permanent qualities. In this way, and in something so simple and common, such as everyday speech, we find ourselves with serious inconsistencies, from the existential point of view. How can we direct our lives, and try to improve them, if we do not even agree with what we are, with what is our own, with what nothing and no one can take away from us? In this respect, it was the conception of the Oriental thought that seduced me.

Buddhism.

It is quite possible that it was too early for me to understand the whole dimension of Buddhism. I think I remember that it did not penetrate too deeply into me, (at least consciously), because this discipline, philosophy, religion, ultimately proposes inaction.

In spite of this, some of his ideas aroused great interest in me. For example, the ***holographic concept of Siddartha Gautama's universe:***

"Truly, I affirm to you that within this very body, mortal though it may be and yet a high ghost, but conscious and mind-gifted, is the world and its growth and decay, and the manner in which it leads to its disappearance." "In a body that is not liberated from passion, nor liberated from desire, nor from longing, pain and suffering arise. The same thing happens with feeling, perception, predispositions and discriminative awareness, body, are not permanent. When you understand it you feel repelled; you don't want it and you are free. Reincarnation has been destroyed, the holy life has been lived, my task is done, and there are no more lives left for me on the terms of this world."

It is in these two ideas that the whole mystery and truth about being and being temporarily seems to be expressed. And I find it curious, as such an ancient culture, was already able to articulate such precise ideas. It is as if they have the ability to handle the laser technique that is used today to operate, but in matters of the soul.

The existence "is", without further explanation, and this is imbricated with the "being temporarily". They are like the faces of a coin, which in this, our universe, never stops spinning. In this way, the whole paradox and possible paranoia seems to be solved simply like this.

Complex to see, if not from an extremely distant point of view, this composition of all things and of being, must have a mortar that makes it palpable to our eyes, to our perception.

*The common denominator, to all this process of continuous reincarnation, is that which provokes the eternal turn of the coin; this is in living beings, suffering, **pain.***

"The enlightened one" says he has the solution to this problem. A solution that seemed to me in the spring of my youth, somewhat disconcerting, and that led to a path full of shadows and emptiness. That's why I didn't pay much attention to him, and to this day, he hasn't been able to calm down the harshness of his ideas, of his path. So, later on, I will return to the philosophies of the East, finding myself fully in the abyss of my "I".

Buddhism speaks, above all, about renunciation. Give up everything, both inside and outside of you. The desire, understood as a wanted or constructed need, as a misleading perception, is unnecessary suffering and pain. But of course, what is necessary to be who you are? How many things can you do without to get to the essence of your being, of your self, and thus to the truth?

The answer is brutal and simple: you can spare them all. And in that state of limbo, or void, is where nirvana is found.

*"What if I, having contemplated the misery of worldly existence, was seeking the unborn, the undead and the supreme peace of nirvana?" "When what is becomes extinct, does the heart feel happy? When passion is extinguished that is **nirvana**."*

A happy, adapted person, with little conflict within him, should not follow these ideas in their hardest form, which only lead to spiritual suicide.

They can be useful to destroy your self, and rebuild it again, reset. Cleared of any prior predisposition, or mental software. This enables you to implement other ideas.

But you have to know what you are doing, or have the right guide, because if it is not very easy to stay afloat, in the immensity of your being. Buddhism is to become a good person, in the sense of gentle, like a lamb, who does not fight before going to the slaughterhouse. It is a vital conception, which neither at the time nor today seemed to me to be very practical, given the competitive and aggressive world that has always existed.

A hostile environment. Not only because of the hostility of the universe, of nature, or of society, but because of hostility towards yourself.

After all, this state of apparent perpetual drunkenness that monks have is not gratuitous either. You must continue to fight internally against Mara (the demon who can express himself within you), to continue on **the right path**.

"I am still in every aspect. This six-foot body is the world, the beginning of the world, the end of the world, and the way that leads to the end of the world." He constantly emphasizes the stillness of the whole within oneself.

"Transient are all things composed. Subjected to decay are all things composite. Striving diligently for release."

With this he emphasizes the movement of the whole, and consequently of oneself. He reaffirms the solution to this suffering, based on understanding this transitoriness, and letting it flow to obtain stillness, peace. Basically, it is a fight against yourself and your nature, which should arise alone, not in a forced way. In short, it is a spiritual suicide.

Remember that you, at that time, had the yearnings, the hopes, the vigour of the naivety of the emerging youth. And this whole last solution, actually, sounded like cowardice to me.

It sounded like an inability to face up to a world that was clearly full of possibilities for me. Having known friendship, love, communication with those around me, I thought it was possible to change, or rather to adjust the world, my world. But for that, I didn't just need to know the essence of things. I also needed a pragmatism that would help me to get to know the most important things in life. I needed a thought that would give me strength to give shape to this idea of priority essence. That's how I found the most passionate philosophy, typical of romanticism.

Schopenhauer and Nietzsche.

These two authors captivated me for their strength and rebellion.

The first one proposes an individual who owns himself, capable of giving meaning from his subjectivity to his life, perception and destiny. This will is what makes up the essence of the universe, and at the same time of each of its parts, of us. In the end, all his thinking seems to end in nothing, literally. I believe that it leads to a nihilism from which it is difficult to escape, without the help of a God.

Nevertheless, I was amazed at the similarities I found in him, with Buddhism, and his attempt to instill a meaning, a purpose.

Nietzsche, for his part, was nice to me from the first moment. Being a wildcard man to all, I was not going to be any less.

So that irrational force, and blunt determination, accompanied me for a long time. Sadly, of all those good intentions, today all that remains is cold, dispassionate, and aimless anger.

He seemed to me to be a rabid dog, lost, self-destructive; proposing a continuous search for **what the human being, his superman, should be.** In his unhappiness, product of the pain of the constant romantic search, he bites and attacks with everything, calling himself antichrist, and renegade of God. I've already said that I liked him very much....

Anyway, it is a practical way to put aside issues of the soul, and focus on the person, on the flesh and blood individual. He proposes the tireless struggle to improve, to adapt, to evolve to someone better.

Aggressive, hard, like a fireball shot in a straight line. A lot of things may have been said about him, but well, nobody's perfect. He already says so. I understand that for him, the search for that perfection, that identity, is what defines you as being:

"I love the great despisers, for they are the great worshipers and arrows of longing to the other shore. I love those who, in order to sink into the

*sunset and sacrifice themselves, do not seek a reason behind the stars, but sacrifice themselves to the earth so that it may ever become **the superman**'s."*

So far, my adventures outside the camp had come to an end, without getting deep into the shadows. With the warmth of the light of life ahead, and the cold at the back of the abyss.

Thanks to all these adventurers I was able to take valuable and practical ideas to return triumphant, renewed energy and hope. I had the necessary tools to be able to dismantle all the foundations of society, its morals, ethics, values, patterns or tendencies...

They also filled me with a high sense of honor, of group belonging. You have to understand, that at that time, I seemed to have a large group of relationships, both with family and friends. My life projects were supported and advised by this type of relationship. I was also growing up, learning how these relationships were articulated.
 To integrate myself, it was necessary to follow and understand the different models that could guarantee a full and happy life. I felt love, commitment, a differentiation of good and evil, and consequently, a sense of duty. I was about 21 years old, and ideas like these helped me get back to camp:

"Until now, I've always thought, it was necessary to keep this scheme within an individual: to remember what he defends, and what he has to become voluntarily, to defend it."

Graphically, it would be the fact of drawing a circle of darkness within you, in which a smaller white circle is inscribed, which is what you love, what you belong to, what you defend, and what you are. A contrasting mixture is established within you.

In this way, you can survive by being adapted, thanks to your dark circle in a context of darkness.

The darkness of the hostility from the environment. Unavoidable. We have been created as individual beings. Everything struggles to exist, and sometimes, the existence of two things at the same time is not compatible.

Even breathing, is a constant struggle. Those who have respiratory problems know this well.... Oxygen, it doesn't just get into your chest. Your lungs must make an immense effort to pull it out of the air. To take away from the lifeless, that molecule that makes you live. To generate life and escape from death, buying a little more time. Breastfeeding you from her breasts. Camouflaged, as if you were one of his offspring. Nourishing your being with the energy of that which repudiates you so much, of that which you fear and flee. Obsecrated in your independence, in the denial of the obvious. Thus denying a part of you, and consequently of all....

"Maybe it doesn't matter so much to remember, to constantly reevaluate, what you stand for, if the right thing is done. *Like obsessive-compulsive disorder, this feeling fills you with discomfort. It's like retracing your steps over and over again, to make sure you're right, that you're still there. That feeling obliges you to give priority the capital importance, wanting to cancel out the rest.*

By identifying yourself with what is most important to you, you always run the risk of getting lost if you lose what you stand for. This is frightening, restless, anxiety-provoking. If you're what you stand for, if you lose it, and you're still there, who's left? Maybe the only way to keep it in the memory, what you are, is the same scheme but seen from the side."

Continuing with the scheme of the circles: the idea would be to tear out the white circle and put it on top of the other one. The dark circle would be imbedded in the evolution of time, space and the rational order of events in the present. The white circle, you, what you defend, would be out of all temporal conception or finiteness, it would be idea, essence, your being.

"You must fight for what should be, but play by the rules of what is. Only when you master things that are, you can change them for what they should be."

The idea must be mutilated, put to safety, taken out of the poisonous reality. Excision is necessary. The only and most complicated thing to be careful about is that this spiritual suicide does not lead you to be against what you were defending in the first place. If this happens, the idea, above sure, will become reality.

And consequently, it will become the enemy of the idea that it should be. (The should be, would be justice, the power of love, the help. Having the duty to respect, being equally respected).

a) The strong, eternal spirit, curiously, is the one who commits suicide with determination, and for the sake of something he considers better.

b) Whoever does not want to do anything bad in reality, to defend the good of his idea, will quickly become extinct. Well, that means he has no contact with reality. This reality would attack him and destroy him by having no defense. He has no strength to kill himself, and he will not change anything, which is the aim of the idea.

c) A strong spirit, but less strong than the strongest. These were one time the strongest. At some point, they couldn't stand the boundaries of reality. They are strong, not by themselves, but by the reality that drives them and has invaded them. They are the enemies of the should be. Their vision, is the same vision of the strong, but they do not belong to the should be. They are hesitant, afraid, and manipulate reality not to be an idea, but to turn it against it. They have resentment for those they once were, and have ceased to be for their weakness.

d) The formation of these stages is determined in a common one. This is not advisable, as it means high energy consumption with low efficiency. The one who gets stuck in this phase, sticks his life fighting with himself without defining himself. He is not bad, but he focuses his attention on himself and cannot change the external reality, only his own, his idea. This is correct, but your domain is restricted to a minimum area: yourself.

*Comparing these states, with that of a seed, it could be seen that (a) would correspond to a **reproductive seed.** (b), to a **non-reproductive seed.** The (c), to an **aggressive substrate**. And the (d), in the case of the **eternal seed**"*

3. The edge of the abyss.

This state so vehement and full of vitality lasted me about 4 years, until I was about 24 years old. But once you're out (I don't know if it's because of the feeling of weightless freedom, or because it's addictive and toxic), when you run out of energy, you need to go out again, but this time much further...

In your head swirled these bellicose ideas, mixed with the concept of a duty, rooted in things you loved, and which should be. Let us say that I believed that the individual possessed a high power of control, originated in him, a great locus of internal control.

In this new departure from my point of view, as I entered the darkness and looked back, I observed the relationships and consequences of the acts of my "I".

Remember how the concept of duty, of honor, staggered. It is possible that there was such fragility, because you did not feel support on your goals. At first, there didn't seem to be much love in your life. In the past, however, your attempts to fit in and optimize the relationships around you, only led to more conflict. It was still too early for you to understand that human beings are what we are, not because of what we know, but because of what we have within. It was too early to understand that the genesis of change had to come through an internal, already existing process. And that this program, or mental software, could not be implemented without the necessary hardware.

The second issue that **weakened, was the question of duty.** What was duty? With so many factions, values, a sense of truth, of the human being, what could be the good to defend? What was the evil to fight? And most importantly, if this was so highly subjective, and you were so alienated, so disconnected from everything, what was your damn idea of duty, the right thing, for you, or for beings who seemed to understand you so little?

Thus, as if it were the return home, as the moth that goes to the fire, as the junkie that goes desperate for peace for a new dose, I went out after the origin of everything to find a meaning. I desperately needed more powerful tools.

<u>**Eternity.**</u>

The question that has always haunted me the most is, "What for?" The "why" of things, of an event for example, is about action and reaction, about the causality of relationships, about the order of events. But if life continues to be asked to the end "why?", you find yourself lost, in a void of meaning."you find yourself lost, in a void of meaning. What is the practical use of life? What good is it to the whole? Is our life an instrument of something superior?

If they were to make a little doll of a nihilist, who would pronounce his typical or more characteristic phrase, this would be ***"for what?"***. Children playing would say, "You have to behave yourself," he would say, "For what?" "To get good grades. And then have a good job. To buy you a house, get married and have kids." With a dispassionate, unexpressive, defiant air, the little doll would answer:

"What for? If you're gonna die sooner or later, and have to give it all back. In a few years, no one will remember you excet punctually. It'll be like you haven't been there. Your works, your genes, your ideas, they will disappear. Even if the history books speak of you, this tiny contribution of yours, to the tiny humanity, will fade into the stupid becoming of creation. Any element, any concern, any life is miniscule, if compared to the whole. Such a contribution, in relative terms, could even be negligible."

Someone clever and naive will answer: "To live fully, to be happy, to enjoy, that is what life is for". I would ask you, if the whole system, or God, wants that from us. And if that's the case, why doesn't he have us designed for it? The atheist will say that no one has made us, that we are who we are, period. But, should the murderer who enjoys and is happy to kill, continue to do so? How, and for what reason, should he stop his impulse, in many cases genetic and innate? Aren't most of our features determined? If it is so easy to manipulate our person to the whim of the idea, why do homosexual people, for example, still have so many problems with such an unnecessary taste as sex? Why don't they become straight? How can, a person who has a thankless job and a lot of burdens to bear, find happiness?

For none of the three, (the murderer, the homosexual, the one who is disgusted with his way of life), it seems possible to change, to magically adapt with a little pill, or a self-help book that only helps those who are already well. And if these things get to change you, it's not you anymore. The change would be so from the root of your being, that basically, you would no longer be yourself.

It seems to me that the kind of happiness that is spoken of in our society is nothing but resignation. And resignation without reason, resignation that benefits others, consumes you, as a form of inaction.

For example: that resignation that leads you to think meanly that you have to be happy with what you have, because others are much worse off than you. Is this how you should be happy, seeing and enjoying the miseries of others? The word that comes to mind for this kind of happiness is more like sadism. Again, the idea hidden behind smoke screens: that to be happy is to have more than just someone...

It's as if several slaves are rowing in galleys. The one who receives four lashes on that day is grateful, because the unfortunate man on the bottom of the boat has been given nine. The guy's happier as happy as Larry. He even winks at the foreman, thanking him for the four lashes he received.

So is our society, on many interdependent levels: work, happiness or well-being, existential coping.... If you can't help but see yourself in the reality of your misfortune, it is possible that if it pays you to do so, you might as well try to kill the foreman before you go to the other side. Because after all, for you, to live that life is to be dead.

Why exist individuals with fragmented souls? Unable for them to be at peace, thanks to an ongoing conflict over wanting or feeling contradictory paths at the same time. Unfortunately, the answer of "enjoying life" was no good to me. Because if I took it as such, and followed it with determination, I would have to become addicted to alcohol, drugs, or lobotomized; thus remaining in a rather unadaptive state of happiness. I am afraid, that shadows are denser than clearings in this important concept, and taken so lightly by our society.

If this is what was sought of us, we would be designed for it, and we would be able to survive, and evolve, in a hostile environment. ***For me, the key is that happiness is adaptation.***

Instead of saying, "Are you happy?", we should ask "Are you adapted to your life? Do you feel good, fulfilled, in tune with the whole, even if you are unbalanced, or in conflict?"

Adaptation, as in the natural environment, depends not only on us but also on the environment. This adaptation will be determined by the means you possess, by the innate or acquired instruments for which you are positively selected.

Adaptation can be obtained through a renunciation of everything, as in Buddhism. But doing this, inevitably puts you out of the environment, out of context. It puts you out of the world, out of touch with reality.

What does the universe want from us? Here will be the answer, since the ultimate truth must come out of the generating system that encompasses everyone; for in this is objectivity.

The different parts of this last system will have only a relative, subjective truth. Objectivity, for me, is the result of the sum of subjectivities. That is to say, it is nothing but an enormous subjectivity, the greatest that the system in question can encompass. In this case, the ultimate total system, the universe, is necessarily subjective in its final assessment. What is objective for us, because it encompasses us, is subjective for the universe. Thus, just as the breadcrumb becomes bread, its subjectivity should have been transferred to us. We may not see it, because it's cloaked.

So, through a deep interiorization, I tried to connect the drop of water of my being to the immense channel from which it came: the river of truth of all, the universal truth.

What does the universe want from us? Here will be the answer, since the ultimate truth must come out of the generating system that encompasses everyone; for in this is objectivity.

The different parts of this last system will have only a relative, subjective truth. **Objectivity, for me, is the result of the sum of subjectivities.** That is to say, it is nothing but an enormous subjectivity, the greatest that the system in question can encompass. In this case, the ultimate total system, the universe, is necessarily subjective in its final assessment. What is objective for us, because it encompasses us, is subjective for the universe. Thus, just as the breadcrumb becomes bread, its subjectivity should have been transferred to us. We may not see it, because it's cloaked.

So, through a deep interiorization, I tried to connect the drop of water of my being to the immense channel from which it came: the river of truth of all, the universal truth.

Imagination and determination were not lacking in me!

Remember how many dead hours you spent meditating on what eternity was.
 It is necessary to think for minutes, hours, days, what is the total stillness of an infinite emptiness in time, and unembraceable in space. When you understand this, you must add up one eternity to another. When you do, you must integrate it into an infinite number of eternities. At this point, it is only necessary to think that at some point, a failure of the system must break all that stillness and stability. And why should it be so, and not otherwise? Why shouldn't the universe be linear? That is to say, that it has a beginning and then an end, in which eternity remains forever, without any change, immutable.

I don't know if my arguments will be appropriate or not. After all, it is a very intuitive procedure. But the truth is that I thought that the proof that this **cycle of creation and destruction was eternal**, was the fact that we existed and were here. *If in the universe, which is the last system, a closed system, there was only one possibility of any error or change, (the creation itself), this possibility would always exist, eternally.*

Even if many empty universes were generated, sooner or later, from this nothingness, one should come out, in which as an error or consequence, without further ado, dead matter would emerge; and after this, life.

If the universe were a bag, in which there are infinite black balls and only one white, I thought that even if it took an eternity of eternities, in the end, the white one would come out. Thanks to the fact that we are immersed in a creation, we know for sure that the white ball exists. And in understanding the concept that eternal is forever, timeless, we know that although there are infinite possibilities, there will be infinite extractions.

Let's say, the infinite traps itself in the concept of eternity. That's just the way it is. For if anything escaped from him, and were not encompassed, that system to which he escaped, would be the concept of the eternal universe. Thus, this cycle would be like a whiting that eats the tail, like the Moebius tape.

Another twisted implication would be, (and surely insubstantial, as all the above mentioned), that this thought could be applied to our life. Foundation of the sense of **Buddhist reincarnation**:

If I, my life, am nothing more than the conjunction of certain variables, from the beginning of creation, a person could think that this order, and even the whole order, was represented by a lottery ticket. This lottery ticket, in an eternal draw, even with infinite tickets, sooner or later, would win. Not only should your life be repeated, but in other universes, you will be the other, you will be in another time, you will be the energy of a rock or the wind...

It was a few years later, when by chance, I found that what I considered so revealing, had much to do with the idea of **Nietzsche's eternal return**, and with the **mathematical theories of the chaos** of complex systems. Or so I understood.

Chaos and order, linked in a becoming, not linear, but by jumps. And I was much more surprised by how intuition, the sense of the human being, could become more powerful than any argumentative or scientific paraphernalia, when it came to giving meaning to the whole.

You felt a chill when you saw this, you finally understood that everything is, without further ado. And that deep down, and ultimately, nothing makes any sense, and it doesn't matter. That's **the edge of the abyss.**

A universe without feelings, without reason or meaning to our use. Cold and indifferent. A universe that doesn't expect you to do anything, because there's nothing to do. It was hard to see that dreadful loneliness of the human being, in which a starry sky is not something charming and magical, but rather, the proof that you are only a by-product, abandoned to your fate, immensely alone.

These ideas, and your vital state, led you to rebel against yourself and against the whole:

"If you are able to understand this in such a crude way, (since in reality all the elements of a system are systems, and intuit the system), there can be a multitude of different reactions: vertigo, nausea, fear, hopelessness, joy because you live eternally...

You can feel sad, because you care what you do, and that only serves to make everything transient. Laughter, irony, madness, anger...

After calming down, settling down, after the terrible journey, all you can do is laugh with a certain longing, which translates into <u>indifference</u>*. You understand that these feelings, unleashed by eternity, are nothing more than another universe created in yourself. And you cry out to the immensity that you have created yourself, that you are the eternal universe, that you are God. You've replicated, cloned, just to entertain yourself. Goddamn it!*

There's no right or wrong, it's not me, smile. Accept the pain, and let it all go to hell, let the devil take you. We are victims of ourselves. Don't complain about the pain, it's entertaining until it's unbearable. We are slaves, yes, but of ourselves. We are free.

There is no such thing as heat or cold, there is temperature. There is no such thing as objectivity or subjectivity, there is a point of view. There is no such thing as good or evil, there is consciousness. There's no such thing as heads and tails, there's the coin. There is no such thing as love or hate, there is feeling. There is no such thing as pain or pleasure, there is interaction. There is no such thing as us and the universe. There is eternity.

Everything is just as it should be. Understanding this is respect. It's the true sense of honor. The only thing you can expect from yourself is: strength to endure, and wisdom to understand.

It's all like a game, with nothing to bet, nothing to lose. Just to hang out, to enjoy, to entertain."

You can see how the idea of honor and duty are broken, whether by a situation of helplessness, by the vision of the abyss, or because my strength was running out. I had always sensed this, but had not seen it so clearly.

So I returned to the camp, my strength renewed but dispersed. Believing that nothing should, and nothing bad existed. Even though I was in my world, among my peers, something inside me kept me at a distance. I understood and was able to manipulate, but I didn't think it was very good to know the truth....

4. Descent.

Within a year I realized the following:

That even if you can, or have the right to do whatever you want, the reality is that not all acts have the same consequences. What a discovery!

Acts that are in conflict will each generate a different kind of pain. So, how can we be free and do what we want without pain, what then is our connection to the whole, and of what nature? It seems that in all this internal chaos something wants to guide us. It wants us to take out our innate pattern, to continue donating the torch of life.

I went out one more time. This time, the mere contemplation of the abyss was not enough, I had to descend along its steep walls, held only by a thin rope. This rope was based on two principles.

One, it was the firm intention to return. The other, was the idea that whatever the pain was, I would have to be strong to endure it to its ultimate consequences.

I would try to solve the puzzle of my soul as long as I had the strength.

In my 25th year, with a job that isolated me from society, empty expectations for the future, the idea that there was not so much control exercised by the individual, and finally, the first signs of maturity, I was able to meditate.

Going over everything again and again, in my uncontrolled and repetitive head, I got a rather coherent and articulate explanation. I came to understand the path to follow, which exists in our being. Although I still believed that human evil was largely due to ignorance, I began to think that perhaps it was part of the individual, and it never occurred to me that it was something that belonged to our humanity...

Definition of all existence.

Life. Death of life, matter. And death of death, nothingness.

This was for me the cycle of the total system of the universe. So, when I refer to existence, I am referring to life and death, leaving aside nothingness. With all that has been said so far, I believed I could assure myself that all existence is nothing but a transit of eternal and cyclic energy. Energy forms everything. Its union shapes matter, and our mind or supposed soul. I doubt very much that without the electrical energy of our neurons, we could talk about being.

This transit is translated into matter as attraction and repulsion. In life, it is translated as pain. That's how the definition came out:

"The truth is that everything is essence in duality, which materializes in the elements of the total system, through a transit of the eternal and cyclic movement of it, understanding it ourselves as pain."

<u>Pain.</u>

Pain is what drives us, to the complex living beings. Either by choosing appropriate behaviors; to achieve the best possible adaptation. Or through innate and instinctive behaviors; in which the non-realization of the impulse will cause frustration, pain. Pain, from this point of view, can be considered as a curse, as a cruel gift offered by the generating entity. Damn or not, pain is beneficial as an indicator that something is not going as it should. It is adaptive to the body, and helps it to achieve its goals by guiding it.

Obviously, a damaged system can give erroneous indications as to the course, or state of the system. I do not propose to embrace pain in a masochistic attitude, it is clear. But it is undeniable that to live life to the fullest, you must accept it.

The universe speaks through your pain. Deep down, all it wants is for you to flow, to transit. (Of course, what he seeks is not entirely up to you. Also intervene the doors, or paths that it opens to you.)

You can stay still all your life in a winter lethargy, but you can be calm, it will make you move, even if it is to the other side. You can also put an end to this pantomime, and rush to the other side, the hard way. In this case, it won't matter either because it'll bring you back. And if you don't come back, the eternal stillness on the other side is more boring than the worst thing that happens to you in this one.

You're going through whether you like it or not. In this explosion that is creation, it doesn't matter if you get fired on one side or the other, because you are part of the explosion after all. So, let each person see what they can or want to do with their life or death.

<u>*All you can do is enjoy yourself, try to be happy, with the price of constant struggle following the pain.*</u> *The pain should not absorb us, as it is only an indicator. Obviously, it has a lot to do with pleasure.*

These paths are so even that they can sometimes be confused.

It is as if a machine is giving error indications, but you reset it and rearm it, aware that it is already working at full capacity, because you need to get the maximum production.
 Pain always accompanies us, but it does not belong to us. It doesn't have to be part of us. Sometimes, it is necessary to endure a large volume of pain. This is so because what we get in return is far more valuable to us, in adaptive terms, than the fact that we suffer as little as possible.

*"Somehow, you have to think that there will always be pain, but **the goal is to make it as painless as possible**. Even if it is reduced, it will exist. Pain is an indicator that something wants to move! Not that it's going badly on target, as I thought. Once you know that **<u>this pain is a need for transformation</u>**, and you have already done what you can, all you have to do is hold on, and let it flow.*

After this, you may think that everything is in constant conflict, fight, and so it is. The attraction and repulsion that occur in the universe, in its endless change and transformation, is existence. Understanding it is what helps you to accept pain, and not to try to fight it. All we have to do is try to reduce it.

The error generates pain, but pain is not necessarily an indicator of pain. **Everything is conflict, everything is war.** *We are warriors, in whose background spaces of peace and learning alternate. These spaces actually serve conflict, for they are a preparation for war, for constant transformation, for eternity."*

It is at the end, where you can see a tremendous sense of struggle. It is possible that I only deformed the argument, for the benefit of a heart still exalted and full of strength. It's also possible that I was right. That the whole process of interaction within us was a constant conflict. That it was a fierce struggle, transferred from matter, with a guide, the pain. Thus, _the norm for this would be never to stop fighting, and to obtain the least pain in absolute terms._

"My only concern is not to worry about anything, and still act."

This idea could sum up what I was trying to achieve: _selfless action_. Acting forcefully, and still not getting involved in the system. A system that seemed to have its own plans, without counting too much on the individual. Enduring the greatest force of the universe, indifference, without it ending up swallowing you up in a spiral of apathy, reluctance, disenchantment, depression.

Being sad isn't bad. **Sadness is adaptive**, in the way that it is a feeling that helps renunciation; it indicates loss, or need for it. It helps to cut away something dear, but its retention only causes more and more pain. But a perpetual sadness can plunge you into a well, from which you can hardly get out: _dysthymia_, a pathological form of your mind, based on sadness.

Fighting, feeling something moving inside you again, that's what makes you come out of the well. And in this fight, no matter how much they encourage you from above the well, or throw you ropes, or try to pull you out by holding you by force, the only one who has the last word is you, and it is up to you.

Even then I thought that if you are dragged out, it is almost worse, because all that light and happiness from the outside will only make you feel more unhappy. You may ask, what's so deformed and monstrous about you that you can't be one of them? This can lead to contempt, even for those who try to help you, or for yourself.

Only loving something from above, a terrible fear of the dark, or a terrible anger, can bring you out. And this is something that can only be born in you.

The well is an analogy similar to that of the abyss, or to the one of floating out of the earth weightless, by excess of flight power (an unpleasant _lucid dream_ that I no longer have a long time ago).

It seems, that what I was looking for at that time, is more or less what I have found today: a form of automatism. This brought me closer and closer to **deterministic approaches**. Perhaps the holistic engine of my thinking simply emerged in a clear way.

The stars do not think, they solve their conflicts of attraction and repulsion automatically. In the same way, plants are living beings, and they do what they do because they are selected and designed for it. The same happens with the animal kingdom, which is only guided by innate patterns of action, dependent on selection and adaptation to the environment. Everyone shapes the universal explosion, without realizing it, without being aware of it. They're all explosion.

Thus, the universal mortar would be automatic. It would be the garden of Eden from which we were expelled. In this way, I refused to believe that being part of creation, part of evolution, we were apparently isolated from it. It is very possible that the instrument that provided us with the adaptation, had at the same time, in its maximum sophistication, the capacity to alienate us from ourselves, and consequently, from everything.

Later, I will delve into the possible external causes responsible for this apparent adaptive failure.

As for how we manage this internal conflict, and how our own "I" can be abstracted, letting the system work by itself, little by little, I gradually discovered the different other selves that we all more or less carry as standard.
 Although it may sound a little schizophrenic, I found different selves by internalizing the different ways in which pain was embodied. Each of these sought something different, and in most cases, their interests were conflicting.

It was represented to me as a meeting table, in which each "I", for different purposes, tried to solve the pain in its own way. These tendencies, which fragmented and at the same time shaped the "I", I called out to them **voices**.

<u>**Voice of pleasure.**</u>

At first I called it lust, but the clear connotation of immoral, or depraved, pleasure led me to change its name.

What this voice proposes to you is nothing more than to annul the pain, turning it into its opposite sign, into pleasure:

"What do you know about pain relief? I can provide you with pure pleasure."

Obviously, if you are enjoying something, your vital pain disappears. The function of this voice is to relieve. And what you get is pleasure, plain and simple.

This strategy, like all strategies, can be very adaptive, and help you to postpone the intense inner struggle. But if it's used in a sustained way, it burns you up. This voice is very absorbing, and requires a lot of dedication. It only brings you back to that world, so that you become alienated from others: your family, your work, your society.

A latte, a candy, sex, a drink, playing the lottery for Christmas, can be good, can help your inner energy, restoring it. But if these activities are carried out in an abusive and uncontrolled way, they end up unbalancing you. Apparently, it's obvious and easy to control. But *from the point of view of someone who desperately abuses pleasure, it's the only way he or she has any interest in life.*
 Hence the apparent contradiction of hurting yourself, being well. Boredom, nonsense, extreme sensitivity, disorientation... are very powerful forms of pain.
 And for these people, either because they have not found anything else, or because the root of their impulse is uncontrollable, it is the only way out they have.

Pleasure is complex, and has many pathways; both on the physical, neural, and mental planes. Everyone has it articulated in one way or another. Their control, no matter how much therapy is done, is not easy. What's clear is that you don't choose what you like.

We live in a society without values, whose proposal of happiness is to enjoy it..., to enjoy it at every moment. You have to be constantly cheerful, and with a stupid smile. Like God knows who told you a joke. It seems that our consumer society proposes the enjoyment of all kinds of pleasures, but with moderation.

To give yourself to the most basic, most primitive delights, and still have a high moral.... It seems to me that this is pure hypocrisy. There is not even an attempt to qualify the purpose of the mass pursuit of the philosophy of pleasure.

Not only is it not hidden, it is magnified. The more superficial, the better, the more practical, the smarter.

I believe that the human being possesses greater abilities than those of trying to live in a perpetual orgy. There'll be someone else who'll do the trick. But I think it's an exaggeration to want to implement it as a model for an entire species.

By aggressiveness I do not mean physical, verbal, or behavioral violence in general. I am referring to the strength that comes from us when we have to face an impediment. In this case, it would be to solve the conflict by force.

"I must dominate, do you want to be a coward all your life? Fight the pain."

Its function is to fight. This voice proposes to put an end to what is in front of you, even your own pain.

In its purest and most automatic form, it makes the pain go away. It does this because it turns your whole being into an instrument that only exists for the destruction of the barriers that impede the achievement of your goals, whatever they may be. Besides, why deny it, we all know that to destroy, to break the barriers that constrain you, produces an intense pleasure. You don't have to feel tied down.

Becoming a whirlwind of fury, and destroying it all around, causes ecstasy in many. The limit is in each one. Knowing which barriers comfort you, give you security, and which ones hurt you, is the difference between a healthy individual and a maladjusted one.

On the bright side, no matter what happens, you'll always act. You will not be paralyzed by pain or fear, which is nothing more than another form of pain.

Then, I thought that the genesis of any recovery, the very movement of the inert and life, were formed by this feeling, that of struggle. This voice, sustained over a long period of time, or executed left and right around you, may generate a punctual movement. But when you run in every way, you end up in the same place. You may end up lost in a sea of rage and anger, without any direction or sense.

You need an orientation, something you want out of the well, or at least something you want. In this case, this voice is necessary:

Voice of the nobility.

"You must leave me control, you're clumsy, you can't tell right from wrong. I'll guide you."

With this voice I was referring to the moral of the subject, to the scale of values (whether or not they coincide with those of society), by which he is guided.

Its function is to guide, to provide a direction in which to act. It is the assignment of values to the elements and relationships that form part of the subject's life or activity. With respect to these signs, the concept of honor arises, whatever the sign may be.

With the defense and search for good, of those who are positive, the concept of **duty** arises, and inevitably included, that of **love**. That's the positive thing about this voice, the love of anything: love of an idea, person, thing, the creator, yourself. The bad: It is possible that you polarize everything in a very rigid way. If you love, you must hate:

You may think you can love everything, but that's the concept of respect. The logical thing is that those elements that are negative should be despised, attacked, or tried to change. Those who are neutral, those who would be potentially positive or negative, would be in a latent state.

Those who defined themselves as positive, and then became negative, should expect revenge.

These reasonings can become implacable and harmful to the individual. The **process of evaluation** should be instinctive, because if it is articulated with reason, if it is not objective, it can lead to a misalignment of values. Delimiting good and evil is a very difficult thing, and more so within oneself.

*   **Morale**, *for example, may not only be wrong at the time, but it will also be wrong in the future.*

A few centuries ago, for example, it would be unthinkable for a black man to be living with a white woman, unless he was not in slave condition. That is, the morality that is appropriate for one age does not have to be appropriate for another. At some point, our current morale will cease to be valid. So, you have to accept that it's not perfect.

What I am about to say is that if in a joint assessment there are doubts, how can it not be even more complex to generate this system internally? In my opinion, the idea of the absence of a god, hedonic happiness, combined with an excessive categorization of the individual, causes this fragmented social reality. Thus harboring individuals atomized and in continuous risk of collapse.

The **categorization** *I am referring to: the same individual is, and can be, many individuals at the same time. By this, I do not mean the selves of the internal voices. I am referring to the cast of characters that we have to represent, in this vital theatre.*

For example, children and adolescents must submit to different systems: parents, school, friends, social networks, idols....

Faced with such a bombardment, not only of information, but also of the requirements of each system, already at an early age, the subject is subjected to a high level of **stress**. This stress not only occurs internally within each system, but also generates a high level of conflict between them as individuals.

So, what values should they acquire, what values and guidelines are common to all their systems? Most of these systems are virtual, and only have value within society, or within the system itself. Only those individuals who are capable of internalising a high degree of conflict and ambiguity will survive or triumph: those who are called outgoing, optimistic.
 Somehow, from the cradle, the individual is already taught to be a **social predator**. It is taught to offer a face, but then to be something else; to say one thing, but then to do another. It breaks the conscience.

This pile of hypocrisies creates a perfect setting for predators of predators: those who run the world, beings guided by the most unbridled ambition.
 I don't know exactly what the definition of being human is, but it's clear that this behavior of our social elite, of our leaders, is more like that of a basic, reptilian animal.

Thus, in my opinion, society would be a jungle, a virtual ecosystem, created by humans to devour humans. The traps, the places to drink water, to which the unwary human being approaches, would consist of fixed and absurd ideas taken for granted from childhood.

This voice, which can be very adaptive when it comes to relief of pain, if it has prejudices or erroneous predispositions, can make you fall prey to the clutches of our society. Restructuring everything can also be harmful. Realizing this can alienate you, and leave you in a blind spot in your social world, in the deepest loneliness.

Those who lie do not feel alone, because they simply believe that it is something intimate and proper. They think they're doing so well, it's totally unnoticeable. Actually, most people lie.

It is difficult for them to accept this, because they also lie to themselves. They are so worried about hiding their skills that it is difficult for them to see each other's skills. They do it unconsciously, and as a matter of course. All actors, all right, all civilized. But when you leave the tedious and laborious task of playing your role, and concentrate on your dialogue, you see everything with a diaphanous clarity. While you're performing, on stage, it's hard to see the flaws in the others, the props, the audience. You merge with your character, you don't see or want to know anything else. And it is logical; that each one plays his role to give shape to such a magnificent spectacle.

<u>Voice of reason.</u>

"You have to optimize your points of view correctly, and to learn, you have to question everything, doubt everything."

This voice is a mere instrument, it studies the variables that affect your life through logic. It's like seeing the picture of your life without the colors that would be the emotions. Therefore, being only a cold and distant instrument, it does not have any kind of propositive function. It has no goals, no guidance. What it seeks is to break and recompose, over and over again, for study, analysis.

Evidently, thanks to this impulse of curiosity, we can read patterns that have occurred and that will occur, even without necessarily having lived them.

The counterpoint to these benefits, is that it is possible that if we use it too much depending on which facets of our life, we end up in a sea of **doubts**. The obsessive doubt of whether you are doing something right or wrong can leave you paralyzed. It's like you're walking around and thinking: now one step, now the other, at this angle... in the end, you're likely to stumble. This "why" and "for what", repeated over and over again, leads to no meaninglessness, to indifference.

It is better to use ***instinct***, *which for me is nothing more than innate or subconscious reasoning, implicit.*
 I have already said that this vital force, this impulse coming from the great creative explosion, would be the form of automatism, the return to Eden, the instinct. By this, I am not referring to the animal instincts existing in the different voices, I am talking about the instinct that arises from the consciousness, not from the underlying impulses.

Finding that instinct is a difficult task, since in each one it is different, because I have already said that human beings are several species within the same one. And if one of the factors that distinguishes different species is the absence of reproduction, the same thing happens in humans.
 I don't mean a physical reproduction, of course. To the reproduction I am aiming at, it is to the reproduction of ideas, of the mind, of that virtual space that we call soul or spirit.

How else can there be very intelligent people, who cannot abstract their ideals and objectives, putting them in a common space and alien to them, for their detailed study?...How can predispositions and assessments made a priori, can make rational beings fight like wild beasts, for absurd reasons, which are not crucial to their vital existence? How is it possible that two beings, with the power of speech and communication, are incapable of understanding, trusting or helping each other, even in spite of living together for many years in an insurmountable solitude...?

This, for example, happens with family members and people closer to them. There is still the feeling that you get when in a crowded bus, you feel in the most absolute solitude, although you are very accompanied.

Most people are not able, cannot, do not want to do, an exercise as simple as listening and getting to know themselves. How are they going to be able to listen, or maintain true communication with another person?
 If they can't even handle, know, the tricks of their inner self. How can they offer trust to others if they don't even have it in them?

It is as if the king of one country wants to enter into an alliance with another kingdom without knowing what his agitated nobles will do. Why else, even with ample information, what happened to others, what happened throughout history, both personal and human, continue to be the same setbacks, over and over again?
 The only explanation I can find is that we move by instinct, or a set of instincts. If this were not the case, we would be able to address our edges much more effectively. And if we assume different instincts, there should be different species. Reason

is not so important, it is not what moves us, it is not what defines us.

Voice of suicide.

"None of the others do anything to take you to the other side, no matter how much you are, do or get, in the end you will have to leave with nothing. I don't help you to bear the pain, I'm more effective, I eliminate it."

Suicide, I say here in a self-destructive sense, the end of which, in its extreme degree, is death. It has occurred to anyone to think that if the key is to endure the least pain, the most logical and certain solution is to take one's own life.

The truth is that for this voice to emerge to its full potential, a great deal of activation energy is needed. I mean, even if you just decide to do it, the other voices will stop you. Each of them will think of something worth living for. Only those individuals who are at zero, or who feel unbearable pain (either from pain, or immense boredom, which is a form of pain), will be able to gather the strength to activate the voice of aggression against themselves, voluntarily.

As ***Sophocles' Antigone*** would say, "And if I die before my time, I call it gain. For whoever, like me, lives in misfortune without counting, how can he not profit by dying?"

Or as ***Hamlet*** would say:

"To be, or not to be, that is the question:

Whether 'tis nobler in the mind to suffer

The slings and arrows of outrageous fortune,

Or to take arms against a sea of troubles

And by opposing end them. To die—to sleep,

No more; and by a sleep to say we end

The heart-ache and the thousand natural shocks

That flesh is heir to: 'tis a consummation

Devoutly to be wished. To die, to sleep;

To sleep, perchance to dream—ay, there's the rub:

For in that sleep of death what dreams may come,

When we have shuffled off this mortal coil,

Must give us pause—there's the respect

That makes calamity of so long life.

For who would bear the whips and scorns of time,

The oppressor's wrong, the proud man's
    contumely,

The pangs of dispraised love, the law's delay,

The insolence of office, and the spurns

That patient merit of the unworthy takes,

When he himself might his quietus make

With a bare bodkin? Who would fardels bear,

To grunt and sweat under a weary life,

But that the dread of something after death,

The undiscovered country, from whose bourn

No traveler returns, puzzles the will,

And makes us rather bear those ills we have

Than fly to others that we know not of?

Thus conscience does make cowards of us all,

And thus the native hue of resolution

Is sickled o'er with the pale cast of thought,

And enterprises of great pitch and moment

With this regard their currents turn awry

And lose the name of action."

Here Hamlet calls being, to resist, to endure. He proposes that courage lies in not being, in taking one's own life. It is the consciousness, the possibility of another existence, eternal and unknown to carry, that holds back that more rational impulse. The problem with believing in evolution is that you don't believe in that immortal soul going somewhere other than nothingness. That way, nothing would have to stop you in the face of a sea of calamities. Nothing to comfort these sorrows, nothing to take responsibility for.

In the face of this, it just occurs to me that it is better to endure any kind of pain, as far as possible. After all, whatever happens, the other side is certainly more boring. There should always be something to enjoy, even minimally. A sound, a taste, an idea.

There may be people or systems that need you; use your life in them. If you're going to throw something away, somebody better take it. Although if the pain of existing is very intense...

The positive side of this voice is that when handled with care, it can, shall we say, prune your being. It is capable of ending those aspects of you, or your life, that need a renewal, an adaptation to the new ecosystem in which you find yourself. Whether it's inside you, or the relationships on the outside.

The downside, of course, is that their extreme degree is death. Within the continuum of its self-destructive dimension, it can also be very pernicious. Risky behaviors such as drug use, obsession with control such as anorexia and bulimia, social isolation, etc...etc. In general, mutilations on a physical or personal level.

<u>**Voice of indifference.**</u>

"I laugh at you all, you see nothing but your little plot. You don't see the whole truth: that nothing matters."

This would be the voice of what eternity wants from us: absolutely nothing. Whether we want to or not, we'll move on. No matter what we do.

Indifference is the most powerful of voices, as it can ridicule them all. No matter how much you enjoy, how much you reason, how angry you get, how much you believe in a meaning, or how much you speed up the end, the truth is that everything will inevitably go to hell.

It can be adaptive, for example, before the need to stop overexerting yourself when it comes to reaching a goal; making you understand that achieving it is not so necessary.
 Besides, the important thing is to be happy, to be adapted. Because in the end, whatever you get, you'll have to give it back. It can help you get up after a failure, showing you that you don't have to win or lose, that you just have to exist and enjoy life.

Indifference helps to recycle. And it does so without the need to destroy, as aggressiveness or suicide would do. It leaves everything forgiven and clean so that we can continue to build.
 She also has great strength: *"Someone who doesn't mind being touched shows more strength than the person who is or thinks is untouchable."* Or, as my grandmother says, *"There's only a problem if you look at it."*

On its most negative side, prolonged indifference over a long period of time can lead to apathy, depression, anhedonia. If one person is continually thinking that everything is the same, that nothing matters, in the end, any kind of motivation is destroyed, leaving the individual in a kind of limbo. It is as if only the body were left, an empty vessel wandering about with no interest in anything, no sorrow or glory.

In my opinion, these would be the most basic components of our personality. In some people, the hierarchy will be established in one way, in others in a different way. This hierarchy will not only proceed in an innate way in each individual, but will also depend on the substrate, on the circumstances that select their behavior.

The return to Eden I mentioned earlier is based on the fact that each of the voices is as if it were an individual based on a single instinct.

If each one of the components of the personality is innate, automatic, if its hierarchy is also innate and selected by the environment or natural environment, it is possible to think that the idea of "I" is only something fictitious, generated by the fact that we can observe the intimacy and interaction of its basic components.

I mean, deep down, we don't control or handle anything. Like the rest of the elements of the universe, we are also driven by that vital explosion. ***We would just be, like the rest of the universe, drifting receivers***. In this way, we are no longer something that is unconnected with creation, but neither we are something special or touched by the hand of God. All this points to ***radical determinism***.

Some people may think that you can change yourself, or that you have a choice. But for this genesis of change to exist, in my opinion, it is necessary to have the required program or software for it, in the voice of reason.

Therefore, some people will innate the ability to redefine themselves, to restructure their internal voice pattern, and to act accordingly.

Others, on the other hand, will not possess this characteristic, and therefore will be flat characters, without such an abrupt or clear evolution. As for the fact that they have a choice, it's more of the same. What you are actually doing is acting, and choosing what has been decided by the ordination of your voices. You can't choose to kill yourself, or kill someone for no reason. A person does not choose to submit to monstrous pain afterwards (unless he or she is mentally unbalanced, or this idea fits in with all the others). A balanced person, right or wrong, will always try to be guided by the "as painless as possible rule". Thus, his apparently free choice is marked by this simple idea.

I repeat that this "as painless as possible rule" need not be a rational concept. It is rather a question of intuition, feelings and sensations. That is why stable concepts (with the minimum risk), are sometimes sacrificed for the sake of more unstable, more kamikaze companies.

Even if it is inadaptative, these behaviors that will later complicate your life, may be done, because without them life has no meaning.

Although it may seem counterproductive to go on vacation for two weeks, spending a month's salary, for many people this is an unavoidable condition for approaching the concept of happiness. Thus, such a waste of money seems unsuitable. But it is only in relative terms. In absolute, vital terms, it will be positive for them.

People with self-destructive addictions will perform such activities because for them, paradoxically, to live life is to make it be consumed little by little. They do what they do because that's the only way they feel alive. These pernicious incentives should be replaced by others that are not, but if nothing is found, or nothing satisfies...

I, for example, have always known that overthinking things and trying to understand the mechanism of human relationships is problematic in the long run. Seeing where something is going, discovering the background of hypocrisy, the falsity of most relationships, will inevitably lead you to isolation.
 But I can't help it, not even by sleeping, unconsciously. Without the whirlwind of ideas and constant conflict, I do not feel alive. So I guess that's all I'm about: someone who's got his mind spinned. And I'm afraid I didn't choose it.

To know where a person should go, it is necessary to reflect a little on what each of the voices ask for. Once you know, as if it were a debate or a meeting, you can get the result that you are more satisfied with each one of them. In each specific situation, or in each life situation, one thing will be required, and one voice or another will be the one to lead the way over the others. The result is applied, period.

It is evident that if any voice has been ignored or assaulted, when it takes control again, it will try to retaliate against the others. Therefore, the more stability (whichever it is, since there are people whose natural balance is instability), the less internal conflict and the more calm it is.

When I was a child, I remember that in my house there was a wardrobe, the inside of which had mirrors all over its walls. When you put your head in there and looked, it was like everything multiplied to infinity. I wondered if they were all real.

Well, we may have seen an interdependence of voices, in the sense that they need each other. *Inside each one, as a fractal, they are repeated and the others exist.* For example, suicide requires aggressiveness to be carried out. The same goes for nobility.

Remember how at that time, your heart was still pounding. The vehemence and passion of your ideas could be seen in lines like these:

"Depression. Does being depressed have its roots in the importance of things? I think at first glance, it's a failed attempt to try to resolve a lot of conflicts. Most of all, I think it is the voice of the nobility that is to blame, in terms of the feeling of responsibility. The voices, their feelings, the tasks they require, are not focused on a correct order of priorities. Many times we try to reach everything, even the least important, and we cannot.

Obviously, when it comes to voices, from a psychological point of view, there is a tamponade of the pain, and an internalization of it, but without processing it.

After this, the voices are blocked except the indifference, which generates the real cure. But instead, indifference finds no entertainment, and turns to the almost always pernicious voice of suicide as a last resource and a way out of boredom.

This only causes more frustration, as suicide needs a high level of aggressive activation and does not find it.

What is depression? It's like lack of movement in a vehicle. With the peculiarity that it has a lot of fuel, a lot of pain.

Here enters the concept of the two senses of aggression: towards the outside, or towards you. This depressive impotence needs to be solved, but *with destruction. Aggressiveness inwards. An aggressiveness that does not mean total cessation. You build or remodel your world, your values. You have undone or redefined objectives that have clashed with your environment and are not suitable, they do not adapt. Hence the pain, but no movement.*

It's like standing in front of a wall and head-butting you. You don't do it for enjoyment or struggle, but because you want to go to the other side inside yourself. The wall is the universe. The other side is the universe. You are the universe. The other side is you. ***If you can't change the world, don't worry, you can always change yourself, you are part of the world. In this way, by changing one component of the world, which is you, you are already changing the world.***

Through this process of adaptation, aggressiveness emerges renewed like a phoenix. This knowledge of adapting to their environment, will act both inside and outside, if they have occasion, with a concept related to duty and corrective spirit: **revenge***.*

When the process of depression has been completed, there are three possible outcomes that depend on the nature of the individual:

—<u>You accept the wall and you are paralyzed in your pain.</u>
 You hear the voices weakly, and you don't make up

your mind or enjoy yourself. It may be the other way around, that by listening to your voices weakly, you hesitate or do nothing. Eternal depression.

—<u>Like a snail, like an existential autistic person, you take your inner world and leave.</u>
 You tend to be sullen, and you try to get away.

—<u>Again you hear your voices, very loudly, but in a different order;</u> and somehow they thirst for corrective vengeance with the change of power, or priority in it.

If you look at it, these are the steps to follow, in the same order described, to get out of the overwhelming situation. In this process, you can stay anchored in one of them.

*Put more clearly, and in reverse order, three choices: **Either you come out of the pit fighting without being the same as the one who came in, or you stay in the pit, or you drown your soul.** In the latter case, leaving the body empty, sooner or later arriving at the inevitable conclusion that it is better to see the universe from the other side.*

The best option: there isn't, it doesn't matter. Everyone will know how much they want to entertain themselves. Pain can be entertaining, if that's all there is at all. In depression, it is thought that pain does not compensate for what we are experiencing. The pain tells you that you live, you have to learn to accept it, to enjoy it. When you enjoy yourself, you are happy. It is possible to be always happy, since it is possible to enjoy even the pain. All pleasure has its origin in pain. Pleasure is to enjoy, to entertain oneself with that minor pain. The other side is very boring.

In depression, all your voices tell you that you're pathetic, because they don't have what they want. Maybe, because you haven't put them up for negotiation."

<u>**Psychological point of view**</u>.

Remember how pleasantly surprised you were when you started studying psychology, when you saw that many of these ideas had a scientific basis, more or less close.

With regard to the idea of automatic voices, and the generation between them of the identity of the "I", I saw a great resemblance to the ***conexsionist proposals***:
 Basically, the absence of a symbolic content, which was managed by a central executive. Besides, the fact that it is the neurons working together that generate the virtual space of our spirit.

Thus, it is not our "I", the idea of an internal homunculus who controls everything, who exercises control. This would only be a mere spectator of the molecular interaction of the neurons, collected in the modules that would be the voices.

It is this continuous feedback, of internal information, and of the medium, that would generate our idea of the "I".

Voices would also have to do with **neural phylogenetic development**:
 After all, just as the first cells included simple components that were beneficial to them, our nervous system had to go through the simplest structures to form the neocortex; this is the part that differentiates us as humans.

That is, if we come from the monkey, and this in turn from the reptile, in some way, those impulses are in us. These processes are regulated by our neocortex, the most evolved element of the nervous system to date.

Thus, in a way, the voices would be modularized in these different types of structures. So that each module, or voice, would have its own adaptive version.

It is very possible that this process also occurs in **ontogeny**; that is, in the development of the individual throughout his or her life:
 The voices of _aggressiveness and pleasure_ would be understood in **childhood**. _Suicide and nobility_ in **adolescence**. Reason would have its fullness in youth. And finally, _indifference_ would have a greater affinity for the vital stage corresponding to **_old age_**.

With regard to the **theories of operational memory**, I also found concordances. This concept comes from the **modal model**, inspired by the **symbolic serial computer**. This means that in my idea of the "I", it can emerge as a product of the parallel interaction of voices. Although the final result is really that of an "I" that needs thoughts, ideas in series. This <u>central parallel "I"</u> is the product of the combination of the <u>serial and elemental ideas of the other "I's"</u>.

The concepts of the "I" must emerge one after the other, while the voices are in constant feedback. This is what I called reaching consensus among them.

This model includes three memory stores: the sensory records, the short-term store, and the long-term store.

As an evolution of this model, the concept of **operational memory** emerges: a component that is not a mere receptacle of symbolic contents. The operative memory plays an active role, being located in the prefrontal lobe of the brain. It can process up to nine digits, elements, (although according to more recent studies, it would be half), and in the best of cases, about thirty seconds in duration, or temporary capacity. If we can apparently process more, it is because we associate some element with a fixed set of them in our mind. It would be the use of mnemonic rules.

Also, without realizing it, we're using our **long-term memory**. This is where I thought the concept of the "I" was located.

One support for this idea is that the practice of prefrontal lobotomy, in the mid-20th century, consisting of surgical separation of the prefrontal lobe, left patients with a distinct, more childlike, impulsive and difficult to control personality. I think it is still practiced today, but only in serious cases.

What was curious to me was that in cases where the patient was depressed, to the point of suicide, the prefrontal lobotomy left them in a childish but apparently happy state.

The relatives of these patients stated that they were satisfied, as the person in question was not absent, not only physically but also spiritually. I imagine that an overly depressed person will be like an empty body so they will not notice any difference in personality. After all, the person had changed, and they didn't notice. It means that they wouldn't know their beloved relative too well in their former state either....

Well, my point is that operational memory, in my view, would be an element like the "I". It would be an illusory concept, generated by the confluence of the different systems of the nervous system and their control. They control each other, and then you get the output, the product as a response.

We would be practically slaves of our most primary components; thus blurring that mirage of freedom.

<u>Concept I had of this operational memory:</u>

Let's imagine an individual, with his head inside a transparent glass box, who would make half a mirror. So that we would be able to see the outside clearly, and at the same time our own reflection not so clearly. This guy, he'd wear it all the time.

He would see on his screen (like the robots or soldiers of the future), different signals associated with the forms and a blurred reflection, like shading, of background, that precedes the rest. This reflection would be you, you'd be seeing yourself. The rest of the elements would be part of the exterior. So that all these images would be included on the screen.

The different elements would each have an indicative signal, colors, and numerical values.

Thus, the colors would correspond to the <u>feelings</u>, the <u>trend signs</u>, and the numbers would correspond to <u>the strength</u> or trend dimension of these signs. Colors, signs, and numbers, would be **like vectors**, communication, the most basic and primitive source of information, that of animals.

The ability to see ourselves would be the instrument that would differentiate us from the animal kingdom. It would be the instrument that makes us special, but at the same time alienates us from ourselves.

This differentiation of the environment, distances us, excludes us from Eden. It happens because we would be able to interpret ourselves in the same way, and fused with the outside. We would see ourselves as just another element, like an animal watching us.

What I am going to say is that this special ability is only because we are the only animals capable of observing the intimacy, the interaction of our ego.

The key point of all this is that we, our self, our operating memory, is not the type we see reflected, in reality, <u>we are only the crystal</u>.

This addition allows us to anticipate not only the outside but also the ecosystem within us. In this way, what we are doing is trying to make them fit together as well as possible; to adapt the internal and external variables. But I repeat that none of these variables are our own. Both internal and external images are alien to us.

There will seem to be a control, but it will depend on what allows us to some extent the capabilities of the person reflected, the data we offer, and the possibilities of the environment.

As an information system (like glass), we inform him. Then, whether we like it or not, he'll do what he wants. Therefore, I believe that the possibility of changing oneself, the component that determines it, must be innate; it is not something that can be learned or added.

There will be those who have a good connection to the inside, to the reflected guy. There will be others who will be unable, perhaps even with help, to redirect conduct that is clearly unpleasant to them. We do not have total control over ourselves, because we are fragmented into different trends. If we had it, we would be guided without hesitation wherever we wanted to be.

It's like we have to seduce ourselves all the time, and if you have to seduce something, it's because it's not yours. Only if the information seduces, or indicates, what is most appropriate for one of the voices, causing it to override the others, will it generate this idea of self-control. I thought deep down, ***we're just drifting receivers***.

The elements of the outside are connected to that vital explosion, to the material universe, and to the man of the reflection. This one, being just another element, is also connected. Our only function is to inform man (I repeat that the action of taking data is innate). The information module that we are, also has a physical, neuronal, substrate. It also has its limitations. Its characteristics are determined by the interaction of the environment and genetics.

In conclusion, this whole process is, let us say, automatic in the sense that it knows what it has to do.

<u>Freedom</u>, would only be the ability to choose options that will ultimately be determined by the "as painless as possible", depending on the degree of flexibility of the man, the mirror and the medium.
This apparent elective capacity would actually

be determined by the interaction of these three elements. Thus, the "I" as the central executive, as the all-powerful agent of his destiny and being, disappears.

Why then does this alienation of ourselves, of our environment, occur? Expelled from Eden, by an angry God, because we have taken something that has made us free, but slaves to suffering. Where do the continuous disappointments, the never-ending longings, the feeling that no matter how much you have of everything, you will always lack something? Why be aware of your finiteness, the fact of seeing your own death on the horizon?

With the question of the voices, the solution that I proposed was the consensus of them, and the application of the response obtained. Doing this without misgivings, with courage, accepting whatever came out, whatever it was.

In short, as a great tennis player would say: <u>"If you do what you can, you are not obliged to do more"</u>. Whatever happens, there is no need to regret what you have done; error, failure, is necessary to get to the right outcome:

A mouse, to reach the exit street, must first locate the closed alleys. In this way, the total circuit (including the errors), would be the one of success. Thus, in the history of our lives, many of our successes are the product of previous failures, without which we would not have taken this direction. You can think: someone might tell this mouse where the exit is. But the truth is that only a mouse can inspire such a concept, not the experimenter. I mean, only someone of your kind can help you. Someone who speaks your language. The same thing would happen with a person.

No one seeks their bad results on purpose (even the masochistic person who actually experiences pleasure). <u>We all do what we can for our well-being, but a bad communication with our inner person can cause interference.</u> These interferences can come as standard, or they can come from the environment, which in our case would be society.

Society is our ecosystem, the environment in which we move. Remember how about 27 years ago, your paranoid mind made you see a strange conception of human association. Something you hadn't even imagined:

Society in its constant becoming, with its different cubicles or ecosystems, would be, so to speak, the punctual moment of a larger and more complex being, **culture**.

Culture and society. I don't know if they're the same thing, or one encompasses the other...

The truth is that we are in charge of giving physical form to an entity that has its own evolution, its own purposes, its own form of existence or life. We shape it, because we don't really control it; it has emerged as the interaction of our thoughts and actions throughout history.

When we are born, we do it with nothing but basic instincts. It is then when society is in charge of violating us, of shaping us according to its own purposes, of shaping our emotional and mental predispositions according to its morals.

It imposes a lot of categories on us, which we have to serve, so that we can have a real representation only on its terms. You are a son, you are a father, you are a man, you are a president, you are (actually "you are temporarily", because it will pass) young, you are a husband, you are of one nationality... Each and every one of these identities has its own manual and its own requirement. Each of them will try to pull you in its own direction, generating a high degree of conflict and pain. Who the hell are you, anyway? What is or should be your order of priority? Which of this identity is true or simply fictitious, if in the end it is generated by a symbolic system such as culture? (Again the multiplicity of the "I's", this time outside the person.)

Culture, even if it is symbolic, is real; it has a genesis, a development, and I imagine that it will seek a goal or an end. It was created from the first moment that the human being had the capacity to communicate with each other. Thanks to the oral tradition, the transmission of knowledge from one generation to the next, the entity that I refer to as culture began to be generated. With the writing, the first database was created in which this being could code his spirit or essence. In this way, it had the ability to be implemented in the children provided by homo sapiens.

Obviously, at the beginning, this cultural base would be used by man to be able to adapt better, to have greater control over his natural environment. I know it is a very radical vision, but I wanted to express it in this way, because it is just as it was revealed to me in its first form.

So, at what point did this supposed instrument that helped us not to have to start from scratch, become something that would dominate us, that would oppress us, and take us to the limit of our existential reality? At what point, something we used, did he end up becoming our lord and master, setting the tone and interaction between us, showing itself to be morally stupid at all times, and inevitably in ours?

I suppose that the turning point was the fact of generating an alternative, equally hostile, virtual ecosystem: **society**.

Thus the human being emerged from the tyranny of creation, and his natural selection, and then placed himself in the hands of culture, and his *social selection*. The point of view I have is that apart from the fact that there are different species in the human being, he behaves in the end like an animal, but a **social animal**.

A social animal is a being that has the ability to manipulate his fellow man, to have a lot of facets and masks with which to shield himself and deceive himself. All this with apparent good intentions, when what he is really looking for is his own benefit.

For example, who would dare to deny how senseless and natural the act of fighting fiercely day after day is, just to be able to put an extra zero on their already many-digit bank account? This behavior only makes sense from the point of view of maintaining a superior status over the rest of his fellow men. Without that stupid fight, they are not themselves. They use aggressive behavior in order to control concepts, things, that a child would easily understand as unmanageable. Reason must self-deceive them, making them believe that they are, and do, something important, when in the end they are only rabid dogs.

The social animal is much more cruel and refined than the animals of nature, which rarely do anything except out of real necessity. But of course, the social animal has symbolic, spiritual needs that sustain its mind. Without food of this kind, we would surely only be bodies in constant wandering.

What's my proposal then? I do not propose to return to the wilderness, and destroy all technology or knowledge. What I am proposing, or rather I was proposing, is to use culture effectively and not let it be the other way around.

How do you know when that interaction is beyond the limits? Just when it starts to burn you at all levels, when it starts to be harmful in your life. It is then that we should begin to question the relationship that is established with what should be our instrument.

It's like sex, alcohol, gambling... they're not harmful as long as you control them, and they don't cause you pain of any kind, or an impediment to developing your life in any way that's right for you.

On a psychological level, from the point of view of my metaphor of operational memory, the solution would be **not to be too carried away by the person in the mirror, the social animal that is reflected in the glass**. Calm him down, telling him that you do what you can to inform him, and that if he dislikes it, he should put up with it. Tell him to do what he wants with the information. That you've already done your duty, and that you wash your hands of the consequences. But you do solemnly place yourself at his service, and tell him that you will always be ready to inform him again. **We're the informant, not the executive**.

Even if we integrate the different impulses, that's the only thing we do; decode and integrate information. The real strength or action comes from the uncontrolled interaction of our voices, or personality modules. They are organized, or will be reorganized, according to the information we give them. And this information will act as a natural selection within our heads; selecting according to circumstances, the strength and direction of our mental gibberish.

With this knowledge I returned to the camp and stayed there for about three years until I was twenty-nine. It is true that these new ideas had taken away my strength and desire to change the outside world. They had also reduced my ability to communicate with people around me. Maybe that's the reason, or maybe it's just that I was getting older, I was growing up.

Despite my progressive lack of interest in the world, I had at least been able to consolidate the idea that I could be at peace with myself. I could be at peace. I had managed to connect with the whole, but at the price of knowledge; of understanding how little our ability to control our internal and external world is.

5. Free fall.

Everything was going more or less well, I couldn't complain. It wasn't going well outside of me, which was still the same, but at least I had eliminated the anxiety. Possibly it was because of the idea that the individual did not actively occupy a leading role in the centre of his vital range; corroborated by the slowness of all my projects.

Perhaps I was more at ease, in retrospect, when I saw how randomness was really the determining factor in all the chaotic interactions that make up our lives. It is curious that most of the great detours that occur in our lives occur by chance.

I think you can choose which skills to improve, which tools to choose. These would be, for example, a healthy lifestyle and studying a career, respectively. But <u>ultimately, the final word is fate. The only thing you can do is to prepare yourself as best you can, for whatever comes your way.</u> If the whole universe insists, you may end up living in destitution and die of lung cancer. You can improve odds, but if you win the lottery, it's because you have to win it.

In addition, by objectively comparing the full strength of the variables we are dealing with, the probabilistic improvement is in some cases scarce.

After all, the probability comes true after a long period of time. I'm afraid life is rather short.

If you are five minutes late to a place where you accidentally meet a person, who will later turn out to be important in your life.... If you had gone down another street, you would not have seen that establishment where you would later go regularly, and which will significantly affect your life...

In short, only a child, or someone with his sights, may be able to believe that he is the God of his whole life. Only someone with a huge ego, who blinds him, can believe that he is master and lord of what happens to him, that he can forge his own destiny.

If you don't think you are a receptor adrift, you seem forced to believe in a destination, that everything is determined in advance. But in that case, if what has to happen is going to happen, then why strive to achieve goals that you would easily earn if it were fate?

These two positions, in their most radical version, inevitably lead you to have an indolent air, to indifference settling in everything you do and are. Logically, someone will say that the right thing to do is to think that some things are decided and others are given to us. I'm not saying no, but the reality is that what you really control represents such a ridiculous percentage that it can actually be dismissed. Besides, even if there were a control, it would be given by our interior, by the guy of the mirror, and he is automatic...

At the age of twenty-seven, I was already carrying thoughts that seemed to want to boycott the little I had left safe:

"In relation to memory, it is interesting to observe how the notion of time is nothing more than a concept; a variable that is determined by the perceptual system of living beings and their capacity to memorize.

In the case of animals that are only guided by reflexes, time does not exist. If only the stimulus-response relationship is given, and this relationship is not stored, it is always lived in the present.

In complex living beings, time may well be a mental construct created by our nervous system. The past is generated by the storehouse of relationships we possess. The future would be given by the combination of these relationships, in an adaptive attempt to be able to predict, control, that stage that does not yet exist, in the vital movement of being. Time is a way of measuring this movement, or action, which is what really exists. At each stage the being changes, it is another being different from the previous one, and from the next..."

This kind of thing I was thinking. Absence of control, chance, illusion of "I".... I don't know if it could be called apathy, but the truth is that my strength was running out, and I seemed to need another shot of darkness.

When I returned to the edge of the abyss to see what I could get out of it, all I could find was something that made me slip completely, without any kind of support. The idea that eventually broke all my previous argumentation, already fractured, was to realize that <u>if the operative memory only lasted thirty seconds, and nine elements at most, that was the present time</u>.

Then, if we are present tense, we are always present tense, since our "I" is formed by these capacities. And if our "I" only lives in the present, and there is neither past nor future, then actually the pain that is felt in the present is not real either. I say this because it is assumed that immediately after thirty seconds or more of the nine elements have passed, there is a new "I", since the old, though it may seem real, has passed into long-term memory.

<u>And if the existence of our being is so short, then it is as if it did not exist either. I mean, pain wouldn't exist</u>.

This matters, because as you will remember, pain was the mainstay, as a guiding formula for the correct interaction of voices. The approach is that if real pain is punctual, because it is present, and absolute pain is illusory, because it belongs to long-term memory, <u>this ephemeral pain can be reset</u>.

Let's say, you can tell yourself, you only have to endure thirty seconds of pain, and the one who comes after you, hold his thirty seconds as long as he can. Anyway, you wash your hands, and you let every single "I" deal with the pain as best they can. If you stop caring about pain, stop caring about movement, stop caring about life, stop caring about yourself.

I still found the strength to keep patching up the mood for at least a year. As far as operational memory is concerned:

<u>*"What if the information is just an energy footprint?*</u>

It could be understood as the testimony of the process of transformation of an energy translated into facts, into thoughts.

In this case, our existence, our mind, is nothing more than a trace of this reality. Our changing body is also a reflection of all the events that have happened to it. Our role in this reality is nothing more than the traces of something that has already happened, and something that will happen. In mental terms, we are information. The authentic reality is that we are just that energy, that it is never the same. We are the change that takes place in it, through feedback with the environment."

Anyway, today it sounds a little empty to me, but well, continuing with it, and analyzing the trap of temporality:

<u>***Immediate problem.***</u>

"If a person remains static in the past, or future, ceases to exist. Which is more real, the animal's footprint, or the animal standing at the site? Both are real. It seems more adaptive to run from the wolf, when you see it in place, than when you see its footprint. If you see his track, it makes sense to be scared and take steps not to be eaten, but you may not even find him.

It seems logical that in order to focus the "I" on the present, it is necessary to solve the immediate problems.

The simultaneity of the past, present and future, (at the individual and universal level), is the real thing. But the only place you can do anything is in the present.

If you can't kill yourself, you have to keep fighting.

The present "I", awakened by its freedom, is aware that it only has a legacy of pain from the previous one. Committed to his freedom and power, the first thing he thinks about is suicide, as the only way to solve this pain. He comes to this conclusion, because he believes it will solve nothing. It'll be like trying to hold something that'll go away in the end. Similar to bailing water out of a boat with a bucket, when the volume of water entering is much greater than the volume leaving. So, the only thing he can do is to bequeath and perpetuate more pain to the next self.

It is possible that this may produce a perpetual state of indifference and laziness, to the point of realizing that the energy needed for suicide is greater than the energy of the immediate problem required to move forward. Being bound, with a sense of slavery. <u>The way to get rid of this guilt is to think that suicide will only generate more endless change. Thinking that the most natural way to reach it, is through the most immediate problem of its predecessors.</u>

It is not necessary to activate the energy of suicide; because when you are falling without a parachute, you are already dead, even if you are not certified as such. You anaesthetize the pain of knowing you are falling, until the inevitable

impact, with the immediate problem, as if it were a drug.

In this way, you anchor yourself to the present, being more energetically economical than gathering all the pain suffered, the one you will suffer, and weighing it down to obtain the energy necessary for suicide. After all, if everything changes all the time, even if you commit suicide, you will one day live again.

The present is the nexus of union of all reality, it is where the change that is real goes. Thus it also makes sense in our memory.

The present is to exist. Existing means being part of life, anchoring yourself to it through the present. Being real implies belonging to a present, past, future and everything that you cannot see in your operative memory.

What you don't see, it's really like it doesn't exist. Whether this is in your daily life, or on a universal level. But just because it doesn't exist doesn't mean it's not real. If you do not limit yourself to what you see, and it is part of your daily life, you are taking your being to non-existent, though real, places. You become light, and this lightness begins to alienate and depress you, because you are not in your present, you empty yourself, you cease to exist.

It would be necessary to be indifferent while you exist; thus acquiring strength and peace. If you are indifferent in total reality, you tend to emptiness, to nothingness.

In a nutshell:

Being indifferent to your existence, and complying with the immediate problem, is how you acquire the necessary automaticity to be happy (what a plant would have), and be connected with the energy of the whole. Returning in this way to Eden, from which we were expelled, by the projective capacity of our operative memory, and its consequent ability to travel in time (past and future).

And when the individual does not encounter any immediate problems? Then we only have to stop, meditate, analyze vital inertias. That is, listening to the innate modularized patterns, which I call voices. This set of actions are also a problem, so resolving them will be your immediate problem.

Of course, there will always be problems, because after one problem is solved, another problem always comes up. Besides, by immediate problem I also mean the little things, like buying something you need, cleaning, cooking, getting the perfect coffee in the coffeeshops... Anyway, entertain yourself. Do not fall into the trap of boredom, which you hardly fall into if you are doing something.

Like when you don't feel like getting out of bed because you think nothing good awaits you that day. Don't think about it, just do it. You get up, and that simple step should take you to the next one, concatenating all of them until they form what in total terms will be your life. That's how normal people usually work.

There are a multitude of past "I "s, and a multitude of potential "I "s, or futures. This range of possibilities, from the past on the one hand, and the range of future "I's" on the other, have a middle ground, where they all converge: the present "I".

The individual anchored in the present is not directly assaulted by the projections of his possible future "selves" or the already consummated "selves" of the past. Each one demands something of him, but in the balanced person, instead of interfering with him by generating mental noise, they guide him on his way to the end.

The ethereal individual is at once in the past and the future, consequently atomized. The pain, the interference, the inability to be automatic, assail him continuously thanks to all the past and future selves. You will be in constant danger of depression or anxiety. If this projective capacity is mastered, more wisdom can be obtained. If not mastered, it can leave you stuck or lost...

A normal individual, living his life without becoming obsessed with what happened, with the fact that one day he will die, or with the ultimate meaning of everything, will be able to cope with it without much interference, and will become more active in the short term. The problem with these people is that they are more vulnerable to a cataclysm in their environment. For the others, it will be more normal to endure any disaster, as they are continually annoyed.

If these interferences are unbearable, I propose to eliminate (if possible) "I's" from both the past and the future. Each of these "I "s requires an allocation of attention, resources, and energy.

It would be like a submarine, in which the terrible fissures it has, require the closure of some floodgates to stay afloat. The captain must decide to drown some men in them, because there is no time. You will have to close one by one, as many as necessary, to maintain buoyancy; otherwise, everyone will die.

Cut with internal or external personal relationships, even if only the captain remains.

Psychologists, I suppose they would say it's not good to be socially isolated, a sign of depression. But I don't understand very well, because you have to be with people who are not of your own kind, that you have nothing in common, and that their very presence causes irritation.

Frankly, seeing myself surrounded by happy, smiling people (as if they were high, or coming from the world of unicorns and rainbows), the only thing it does, is to want to blow my head off even more.

I doubt very much that happiness will enter by osmosis, with only the approach. You may be tempted by the hope of being like them, but when the hope is over, or you realize that you can never have happiness like that, the result is much worse.

Also, if your strength is at its limit, in order to open doors other than the ones you have, which may give you relief, you need to close some of the open ones."

This formula, the immediate problem, can be interesting when it comes to moving forward, for apathetic or depressed people.

6. In the abyss.

Thanks to this type of appreciation I was able to continue for a while, but it was brief, only one year. I was falling, and my attempts to find a spot to hold onto were totally futile. Falling and falling, more and more.

It is difficult to be in this situation, because when you find yourself in the deep well your life is becoming, it is as if you were not seen by anyone.

You've changed, you have the same body, but you're not the same. No one seems to notice. Maybe some people in your inner circle will.

But all those you used to consider as close, even familiar, if they don't notice, is that they've never really gotten to know you. Maybe, they didn't even understand you. If this is so, it's like they've never been there, and in that case..., What the hell pantomime have you been living until then?

You feel that your life has been a lie. You see the camp from the darkness of your soul, no longer as a longing, or something desired, you observe it with resentment, distrust.

Having been, all your damn life trying to belong to that place, most (if not all) of your goals have been within it. Being angry with the camp, you are also angry with your goals, still within it, and logically, with yourself, since you were those goals.

There is a break with the part of you that belongs to the camp, and very possibly, after a period of inactivity, feelings of self-destruction will occur.

The cycle that I am going to expose, of **internal** and **external aggressiveness**, with the periods of **lack of vital inertia**, would seem to be prior to the _construction of a new self_, with different purposes and ways of facing life. In some people it will happen more clearly than in others. It is also possible that some of these phases may not occur.

In either case, what I have observed, at least in myself, is the factor that has been given as a formula for personal growth, or maturation process.

Logically, in each of the stages, this process has taken place gradually. From less to more. They have been produced with increasing intensity and crudity. Besides that, these stages do not have to be homogeneous, it is possible that some of them contain traces of the others.

So at the age of thirty, you're attending the biggest life shock you've ever had. It may only be the crisis of the forties ahead of time, but the truth is that to contemplate the exhausted camp, after falling face down at the bottom of the well, and the fact of not wanting, of not finding the strength, or sense by which to return to the camp, opened my eyes to a hidden reality.

In this way, being more effective in the camp, with the concept of cooperative predation that is deviously wielded there, the idea that perhaps it was better to create a camp in the abyss, surrounded by creatures similar to me, was drawn into my mind. Just connecting with base camp, to get what was needed out of there.

Let's just say I thought, maybe I should do the reverse process that I had done up to that point. Instead of striving to belong to the place that didn't seem to accept me, or to be mine, I should strive to place myself in the place that was always repelled. Why shouldn't I be able to live happily there too? Aren't the Eskimos, or the nomads of the desert, happy?

These are the streamlined steps, which led me to it, the parts of the overall cycle of rebuilding every person:

— <u>External aggression.</u>

This phase occurs as a consequence of observing what you are supposed to be fighting for. Logically, the computation of lived or imagined experiences will always be greater at the age of thirty than at twenty, for example.

Attempts to find the right place have supposedly led the person to search a wide range of people, situations or sensations.

The happy or adapted person will not have to look for too much in the limited range of possibilities offered by our complicated society.

Analyzing this repertoire of experiences, from an increasingly distant point of view, provides you with a wealth of data, which, correctly associated, can provide you with the patterns inherent in people, both inside and outside, in society. I do not mean to say that it is necessary to go through certain things in order to decide, to learn about what we are and about our lives. You can learn by yourself, without help, a sport, to drive a machine, to study a career.

But it is indisputable that if teachers or experts in the field teach you the basic procedures, you will evolve in a much more solid and fast way. If I had been taught this point of view, the one that was mine, the crudity of my reality, the result would have been very different. Maybe I'm wrong, maybe

I'm not. What matters is that it's okay with me, and it's possible that tomorrow's worth it to you.
When you read this again, I hope you have a more positive view of the rules and nature of society.

<u>**ALL RELATIONSHIPS ARE A SHAM, FOR THE VAST MAJORITY OF PEOPLE**</u>.

"When one observes the behavior of people, as a human ethologist (i.e., as if they were animals), it is curious to observe that it is not the ability to socialize, or communicate with one's fellow human beings, that distinguishes the human being from other species that also socialize.

*What differentiates human beings, and makes them unique in the animal world, is the fact that they carry a **briefcase full of masks**.*

The ability to create a symbolic world of one's own, is used in this case to shape a set of personal identities (I do not mean voices), with the purpose of fitting in as well as possible with a particular interaction. In this way, you can get the most out of this relationship.

That is, basically, each one carries his or her own briefcase with the largest and most varied number of masks, in order to be able to deceive, seduce and traffic, almost always for his or her own benefit. It looks like a dialogue of sea bream, as if there were no real communication. A whole group, or two people, may be talking for hours, but they're really just listening to themselves, worried that you might notice a lot that they're faking. Each one, in a kind of macabre game, tries to get something out of the other while patting each other on the back.

This is the case of the guy who goes for a walk with his girlfriend with his briefcase, and for the occasion he wears the mask that forms such an identity. For work, with family, with lovers, with friends, he wears another one. Each of the masks requires attention and resources. Each of them involves different roles, activities, and behaviors. The masks usually ask for only one thing in return, apart from requiring more and more attention: that there is no interference between them.

They don't like interferences, because they find it offensive, like an aggression within themselves. They are not like voices, because masks are a complete identity that is nourished and shaped by the standard mosaic of voices.

Most people in our society are not used to being alone with themselves. If you think about the intimacy of your being, you may discover the personality fragments that make them up: independent, unconnected, without a common feeling that defines them.

Or maybe they are afraid to look at their real self, at their real face, which is where the rest of the masks fit and take shape. They may no longer have a real face. It will be because one of the properties of these masks is that if any of them remain for a long time, they remain stuck, forming part of the face. Coupled, in some cases in such a way, that it is already impossible to take it off.

Obviously, if the use of masks is very continuous, removing and applying them will wear away your normal face. That way, you can only see in it a terrible blur of expression.

I am not saying that this is a bad thing, because it is, after all, a great source of adaptability. I believe that this concept of mask management is what in psychology is defined as <u>extroversion</u>.

Either way, I think the people found in the abyss will have a very small briefcase. Not for pleasure, but because it's probably given out as a standard. It's also possible that you don't have a briefcase, so in reality, you always go with your original face. This can be quite disconcerting to the people around you, for the simple reason that they think you're wearing a mask like everyone else. There are many conflicts, because, as I do, you cannot split your different "I "s, because you always tend to look for an integrating meaning.

Other people may think you're evil. They believe that this inability to develop the most important of social skills is purposely, proudly and arrogantly despised.

If the voices that make up your identity are so strong that they tend to destroy each other, those identities you generate will also tend to destroy each other. The masks would attack each other, and instead of being adaptive, it would be disastrous."

FULL COOPERATION, COMPETITION, AND COMPETITIVE COOPERATION.

"I believe that the structure of our human society is shaped by these three types of relationships. Cooperation, for me, is the union of two or more people to achieve a common goal or goals.

*The first, **full cooperation**, would be based on unreserved cooperation, where there is real and constant mutual support. The resources of the elements that make it up are free, and are at the full disposal of those who require them. A maximum degree of trust and respect is given. The different elements would function as a single entity, even if they are different and perform different functions. The participants would be guided by a common sense and common goals. There is real communication, and there is the capacity to* *sacrifice yourself for the benefit of another, or for the general interests: today for you, tomorrow for me.*

*The **competition** would be the fact of damaging your opponents as much as possible, as they would all seek the same goal. Each element or individual would be within himself, concerned only with the achievement of his goal.*

***Competitive cooperation** would be a combination of both. Let's say you would have to pay a fee for resources and attention; to work together to achieve the goals. Not all doors are open, as they would be in full cooperation. The limits and actions to be taken are agreed upon, either explicitly or implicitly. Individuals are alone, but there are points where the encounter arises, and it is in those points that they cooperate. In this way, even the fiercest of enemies can cooperate and help each other to a certain extent, if this is in their best interests.*

It is this last type of relationship, which I believe is developing in our society, but with a peculiarity:

Everyone tries to make the rest of the world believe that they are leading a fully cooperative relationship, when in the best of cases, they are leading a cooperative-competitive one.

This is the case with many friends or family. Sadly, it also seems to occur in couples. Nowadays, with individualism, you can't really bet on someone, and forever.

They talk about love, they care, they want what's best for you. There may be only a few, if any. Deep down, they go about their business.

*The whole social fabric, the dense moral tapestry that surrounds us, seems rather generated so that the most skillful people can take advantage of the unwary; that either because of their ignorance or their good hearts, they fall into the web of those who pull the strings.***Normally, behind an independent and highly effective person on his own (if he swallows the story), he will be surrounded by a lot of people who, like leeches, will take away what he produces, for the sake of mutual and reciprocal love.**

For example, we only have to observe that this is usually the structure that is given in stable couples, that are interdependent among themselves, those that have to share resources and strategies.

So is the world, in which there are many lies, but you can only be free, or happy, when you follow your own lies.

This is what masks are needed for. <u>One example is the animal kingdom, where only those animals that cannot fully adapt on their own, make society. I</u>

<u>mean, **we rarely love each other, we really need each other**</u>.

So, for the one who finds himself in his particular abyss... Isn't it much better to be alone than to be in bad company? Isn't it better to take advantage of that intuitive distance that alienates and disconnects you from conventional relationships, to get away from them, not only spiritually, but physically? Why play with a football team that doesn't understand you, doesn't respect you, hinders you, has an unstable game in which you can't lean on, if you can only catch the damn ball and put it in the other goal...?

<u>*I suppose that for someone who has trouble surviving himself, in his despair, it is terribly difficult for him to cope with the ambiguity of a lot of relationships*</u>*. Someone without a mask case will always try to simplify and integrate not only himself, but also the outside in one sense. Therefore, having to constantly define the limits of a relationship with a tug-of-war will be tedious, tiresome, insane, depressing.*

<u>*In seeking something stable, these cooperative-competitive relationships, if not well defined, will be unsustainable, and a product of great anxiety and pain*</u>*. It will always be better to compete, or cooperate fully, in the event that a real relationship is desired. He can also cooperate competitively. To do this, all the terms of the relationship will have to*

be defined beforehand, unambiguously, without lies."

If you think that this is more like the scenario of mafia relations, or of people surrounded by extreme or hostile circumstances, I invite you to do a simple exercise:

You can imagine, that suddenly you have a terrible illness or an accident and you are terribly disfigured. How many people would continue to stand by you? How many after falling into a dreary, stinking, frightening pit would be able to do everything they could to pull you out, even to get themselves in? How many, at least, would try to encourage you by looking into the pit, keeping you company from above?

The stark fact is, most people wouldn't even miss you. In fact, they probably wouldn't even notice you fell.

These harsh circumstances are not the trigger. They are only the light that illuminates the shadows of the true nature of relationships.

It's not that people leave you, it's that you've never really been with them. I imagine that in those who have this social cloud of ambiguous, unstable, fickle and volatile relationships, what lies at the bottom is an undeniable fear of loneliness. They know what's what, they know this truth, but they prefer to try to deceive themselves. Like the one who recites a sickly, compulsive prayer, or who intoxicates the clarity of his mind with drugs to relieve pain.

It is not for nothing that loneliness is one of the most difficult things for human beings to endure, to tolerate. We are by nature social animals. Isolation can drive you clinically insane. Obviously, I'm not saying that you have to look for solitude, and that only the strongest get it. Loneliness is not a dish of good taste for anyone, even when your place is in the abyss.

What I do say, however, is that for someone introverted, on another wave rather, loneliness is more tolerable. It might even be nice.

For these people this option is much less painful and conflictive. This is because they are incapable of denying the truth that characterizes them, torments them, and gives their lives at the same time, by shaping their vital essence.

These people, they have a much richer inner world. In this way, thanks to their recurrent and stereotyped thinking, they can have a real interaction with what they analyze or study. The character in a book, or that variable they try to find, memories of the past, or imagine alternatives to the future, can become more stable, more rewarding and closer than people, or the real world around them, immersed in the boredom of every day.

Besides, just by being who you are, you can find company of your own kind.

The one who goes with priests will always be associated with religion, even if he is not religious. The one who goes with pirates will always be seen as a mischievous rogue, even if he is a saint.

A rhino can cut his horn to look like a hippo and relate to them. But if the rhino then realizes that he doesn't belong to the world of hippopotami, when he wants to return, he will have to wait for the horn to grow.

If your social space is uselessly occupied by people who are not like you, who do not contribute anything, it will be difficult for people who are interested in you to enter it. Even so, if it remains empty, at least you won't have to watch out for non-reciprocal favors, annoying social events, or having to violate yourself, playing a nauseating role, because it's supposed to be done. If the social cloud brings you nothing but problems, and you are able to cope with loneliness by moving away from this cloud, you always win.

It is evident that by loneliness I am not referring to total isolation, like that of a hermit, but to the fact of having few, but sure, relationships. The fact that they are few seems to be a necessary condition for real relationships. Because you know, "The one who embraces a lot, doesn't squeeze a lot ".

"I'm not saying one model is better than another, they're just different. Everyone will know which one is best for them, and which one they are most comfortable with. This will be fine as long as you know what's going on, but the truth is that there are many people who live this illusion in a rather unpractical way, so that sooner or later they fall on their faces, wondering how such a misfortune has happened to them.

Our ego makes us think we're special. We therefore believe that this is not going to happen to us, because, deep down, we are really loved.

It all seems to come about because most people are satisfied with having an "I". This "I" is dedicated to inter-connecting the different worlds of which it is composed. Their central self need not integrate disparate worlds.

They have an "I", in the bottom empty, without being the central executive, dedicated to connecting and cleaning up all possible influence of some worlds on others.

Not having this "I", as something central or integrating, they find themselves not only alone with respect to the people of their worlds, but even before themselves. Surely they will not be able to create an integrating idea that will make them feel they are on a defined course.

What are you going to do? If you're an idealist you can feel good and accompanied by yourself. Instead, you will surely find yourself in dissonance with others. On the other hand, if you are pragmatic, you will feel accompanied by others, with whom you will share ideas. In return you will feel alone with yourself, even frightened by the nakedness of your being.

For me the choice, surely forced by my nature, is clear. I'd rather stay with myself, with my madness.

Every time, the real world seems to me more like a madhouse, with people running around aimlessly, deceived by meaningless ideas, and a logic that gets nowhere. The madmen, they know the truth, that everything is chaotic, that nothing matters, that no matter how much you run like a crazy rat, you won't leave the labyrinth, nor will you solve anything. To live the truth, then, is to be crazy.

From my point of view, the balanced relationships that normal people normally have, would be like **Frankenstein relationships***:*

A social world that seems to be alive, because it is moving, but that in its depths is dead, because it is formed by fragments of dead relationships.

Most people, and more so today, resolve most, if not all, of their internal conflict, giving each part of their personality a different world. They make an amalgam of social relationships, with nothing in common except themselves.

Apparently they are adapted, as they give their voices what they demand separately. They seem to have life, but it is only in appearance, since deep down they are empty and meaningless relationships. In these relationships everyone tries to hide the rest of their world. They seek to get the most out of being with others, without really caring. It is difficult for them to become really interested in any of these circles, as they will always have that other inner friend, which is themselves, to whom they will commit themselves.

If they all do the same thing, they're really alone. And that whole background of hypocrisy and appearance is just an illusion.

They may feel even more alone, due to the fact that no matter how good they are in cracking their system, each of these bits, pieces or subgroups must pass through a central voice. In this way, these interconnections, being in the station, must leave some trace or residual interference that affects the long term. The separation of the different worlds, over time, is not as aseptic as might be expected.

Like when, unintentionally, wearing a mask, some characteristic of another mask comes out automatically, without your wanting it. (For example, the one who is with his girlfriend on the beach, and names her in a different way, since he has just been with someone else. Little lapse....)

This interconnection must create problems of consciousness, or rather conflict, since all these worlds, being so disparate, will try to destroy each other, not only internally but externally. Strange individuals within you, will always be more important. (If they themselves are not stable, and cannot help themselves, how can they help others?). And if everyone does the same, then everyone is alone. They will never be able to help, to give something important of their being, other than emotional alms. Almost everyone seems to simply want to steal and cheat as much as possible for their own benefit."

So, who might be able to have a real cooperative relationship? I think only those who know how to love will be able to do it. And love is not obsessively infatuated with something or someone. To love is to be willing to give whatever is needed to save the target, or loved one.

To be able to love, you must not fall prey to your fears, because people who are, are not masters of themselves.

The fact of being afraid of losing this or that, of not being able to face, even death if necessary, for what one loves, does not make them free. It will be their fears that will set the tone for their lives.

These people will only be like puppets, whose strings will be pulled by the social, physical, or symbolic system that inflicts terror on them. They will be an extension, an appendix, like the arm or the hand, of that which dominates them. They will not be free to love, for being part of that system, they will be the system.

The key to being able to cooperate fully is the ability to harm yourself, if you believe it is necessary, for the benefit of that loved one.

<u>**YOU ARE JUST WHAT YOU CAN CONTROL. EVERYTHING ELSE IS JUST PROBABILISTIC CHIMERAS.**</u>

With respect to goals, it may be best to be indifferent to them. I referred to this earlier, and I am not going to say anything new.

We must be aware that many of the goals we set ourselves in life do not depend on us.

So, don't despair if you don't get them, or unforeseen events arise, because we are not gods, only supermonkeys.

Our society, for its proper functioning, tries to make us believe otherwise. Let us say that <u>we are taught to live in hope</u>: "When I get this, then I will get this other, then I will be happy". And while you're thinking that, mentally, you're already enjoying the ***anticipated reward***.

Like when the rat goes through the maze and starts to salivate the food, recreating itself with the imminent delicacy. But what happens when the rat arrives at the place and is told to go somewhere else, since there is nothing?

That's what our society does. Most of the time, you're just buying a lottery ticket that you may or may not win. But if you read the fine print carefully, no one really makes any assurances, nor takes any responsibility.

"Take care of yourself, and don't drink or smoke. Eat healthy and do some exercise. But we can't guarantee that you won't die an agonizing death from a terminal illness...; it will only reduce your risk."

"Study, so that you can continue studying hard, and then, after investing a lot of time and money, you may know someone who can plug you in for the job. "Hopefully, you'll be able to keep the job, and earn a salary commensurate with what you've invested."

That's the way things should be said, but of course, how many unwary people would stop being devoured by the system? Only those people who have remarkable power or control over a given system are able to obtain this reward in a real way, and not just the illusion.

In our human ecosystem, not only those in the bottom of the social food chain, but those at the top would be like small donkeys. They would all have the peculiar characteristic of having a stick and a transparent thread from which a carrot hangs in front of them. That carrot, would be the vain hope.

HOPE, FEAR AND RESPONSIBILITY: THE THREE PILLARS THAT PREVENT A PERSON FROM BECOMING BLURRED.

These three axes would be the ones that would connect a person to our society, to our real world. In each individual they would have a different force, shaping their characteristic vital inertia in the summation of the three axes, as if they were vectors of movement. As nails, they would be the ones that would prevent the person from rising to the sky like a balloon, floating and moving further and further away from the world, and from himself.

Hopes are important because they lead and guide you to goals.

Fears are also very important, and they are very adaptive, as they can prevent you from behaving inappropriately against others or against yourself.

Responsibilities make your life useful and practical: children, work, those who have supported and helped you, in front of a god, etc. Many people flee from responsibility as part of fear. Others do not, as a result of not having found the person, or cause, to whom they can commit themselves or give their lives. It is logical that they do not commit themselves to what is wrong with them over and over again. They feel in an existential void, which none of these failed, faded, false, insufficient proposals seem to be able to fill. It may be for a high level of exigency, but everyone is different.

I say this, because our society tries to fill these three spaces to have control over the individual, to take shape as an entity, and to make the person an extension of it. If this were not so, everyone would be free. But this freedom, being weightless, is more painful than this kind of slavery. That's why, deep down, freedom is scary.

What I do say is that if we are made to be slaves of something as a requirement to take shape and not just be air, it is preferable to be slaves of ourselves. Being a slave to the system, for some people, can be highly satisfying and enjoyable. But frankly, I don't like the space this society seems to have assigned me. All this is about the fact that....

... SOCIETY GENERATES GULLIBLE, OR AS THEY SAY, OPTIMISTIC.

When I was a little boy I swallowed the tooth fairy thing; it seemed strange to me, but I swallowed it. Santa Claus didn't work anymore. I didn't quite understand why the people who protected and cared for us had to lie so fantastically, and for no reason. I thought, it might be to make fun of us.

Maybe these little lies are for the children to keep their innocence. Or maybe it's to give them hope, and to learn that it's natural, to realize that it was all a farce.

It may be derived from an ancestral way of preparing yourself for life.

In either case, far from diminishing the importance of this kind of deception, I was pointing it at my little head.

Thus, having a job that is inconsequential and unstable at all levels, a mortgage until death, with an ex-wife, and children who end up being strangers, among other things, does not seem to me to be the panacea that can be administered to everyone, of happiness. It will work for some people...

From the cradle, in most societies, the individual is indoctrinated to have hope, fear, and optimism in the face of adversity.

Fear of a god, of morals, of conscience, of having useless things that according to them are essential, of death, of loneliness. It is an attempt to endow the individual with a will and control that he or she does not really possess.

Like in political elections, which at best, the only thing you can do is change the one who had been stealing for another one. Of course, there will be differences, but these are so insignificant in the international and business context that we cannot appreciate them.

With this mirage of control by the individual, our societies avoid the tedious and costly task of subjugating the individual to force. After all, as I heard I don't know where, the best scam is the one in which even the scammers, far from pretending, believe in it.

In this way, the social entity is assured of having its individuals imprisoned and enslaved. They will respect it, thanks to their fears. And they will idolize it, thanks to their hopes; materialized in the eternal carrot, which pushes the donkey to follow it forward, to the point of exhaustion.

Like any suspicious system, it will have a system for detecting and eliminating intruders or harmful agents. Those who have no fears, hopes or responsibilities will be called sociopaths, madmen, hermits.... and maybe with good reason.

When you realize that you owe nothing to anyone, when you feel that you are abandoning everyone and that everyone is abandoning you, when you abandon yourself, that is when the **responsibilities end**.

When you see, in perspective, the value of a life in relation to eternity, what is really enjoyed or lived, you realize that it is worth very little. It is only worth the little treasure, or garden, that each one has. Then, when you realize that you die in routine, in sleep..., you realize that dying would not be so serious. Because actually, it wouldn't be so horrible to lose that little thing you have, and that you will lose someday. That's when **fear leaves you**.

Observe after a while, how much you have controlled; what you have gained from your effort, what it is worth. That life always asks you for something more, to make you worry about it and be happy in this way. That's when you cut the carrot string. Fighting is an relief, not the achievement of a goal or an end. That's when ***hope abandons you***.

Without these three concepts, you are weightless, suspended in space.

THE ILLUSION OF OPEN DOORS.

One of the tricks of our society is to make the individual believe that he is free to do what he wants. In the sense that with effort and dedication, a person can be what that person wants, have what that person wants, be who that person wants to be. It suggests that the person is the master of his destiny.

It is evident that without this fictitious stability and magical powers with which society wants to invest the best of the monkeys, society and the world would be very different.

People would be more aware that the only thing they have is their present moment; and with that, it is what they should count on.

There must be an orientation, of course, and plans for the future, but what you can't do is believe that something is going to happen to you for sure. The fact that we are actually stumbling through life is not only annoying, it can be frightening for many. But, well, that's the truth.

You have to be a little more impertinent, a little more irreverent. There is someone who wants to live to the age of one hundred and thirteen to begin to enjoy life after retirement. But with hard work, in shifts, it is very likely that the state will not spend a lot of money on his retirement pension.... That's as long as he gets to retire. And more importantly, by then, as things stand, the state should have money. One minute, they vote on a law, and everything falls apart.

You have to make plans, but realistic, with an acceptable percentage of success. I don't understand how in a culture where people are getting smarter and smarter, we don't know how to add two plus two. I imagine that coercion and brainwashing from an early age are the order of the day. Indoctrinated in schools to behave well in front of authority, and never to rebel so that they can act the same way in life. They should bow their heads and accept with a smile, pretending that their pathetic life is going well.

In all ages, in all societies, slaves have always existed. They are people in the lowest stratum of society, busy with their efforts to sustain those above, providing them with more freedom, power, and well-being. As time goes by, they are given a different name, as if to wash the concept away, with euphemisms. Today, they would be the people who do the hardest and lowest paid jobs.

It is existentially hard to dedicate your life to work for something that has no substance, no basic need component. It's hard to give your life's effort to get goods and relationships that don't really suit you or come to you, even when it's well paid.

At least, in ancient Egypt, the slaves who died and worked in the pyramids were told the story that when they died they would reach the glory of eternity together with Pharaoh, and that their work could be admired throughout the ages. Today, in the culture of wellness, you perform tasks whose result will not last long beyond a garbage can, or your memory: washing machines, car components, serving coffee, selling useless products... etc.

The tale that is printed on fire is that you have to enjoy life.

The slave is coerced, to spend 15% of his annual salary in a week's journey, you know where..., to spend 20% on private vehicles..., 70% on a mortgage, for a house that won't really be his, until he finishes paying for it, on the verge of death....The bills don't come out. Does it seem logical that a person can be paid like 7?

Someone might say that it is normal for him to earn more because he does a much more important job, without whose performance, the other 7 would not be able to do theirs. But I would tell him my view of the subject with the analogy of a house:

The roof is certainly very important, because without it, there would be no house. But even more important are the foundations, because if they are not solid, no matter how beautiful and expensive the roof is, a simple natural inclemency can wreck it. The roof can be fixed with anything..., even branches, and over time, it can always be changed. But once the foundation is laid, there is no turning back unless everything is destroyed; that is why I think it is more important; if true, that both components are needed to create a house.

That's how society looks to me, what's important are the individuals on whom it is based, because if they fall, everything collapses.

If these kinds of inequalities are not what they are in a hostile and competitive system, you can tell me which one. And if in such an aggressive system, there must be predators and prey, it is common sense that in social terms, the prey can be called slaves.

It is difficult to realize this, because nowadays when you are born a slave they indoctrinate you as such, making you see that you are not. In the old days, the line was more defined. If you did not have the courage to die for your people, to avoid their conquest, the punishment or alternative that awaited you was clear, to be a slave. From this perspective, the fact of making slaves is not so cruel; nor is the fact of being a slave, so victimizing.

The doors or barriers of our social system seem to be open, but that's like when you want to get into a party:
 You get to the door, the doormen tell you you need a ticket. It seems logical, so you spend a lot of your time and resources getting the ticket. When you get it and come back, they tell you you can't get through yet, because you need a suit. You see someone walk by effortlessly, and dressing as he pleases. When you ask, they tell you he's passing because he knows someone, or he's a VIP customer. If they always ask for something more in return, it looks like they're not going to let you in.

In this type of system, individual competition prevails, as if access were a funnel. They show that all elements have the same opportunities, but in reality they do not.

Thanks to this veiled lie, the injustices of the system are less evident, bringing greater stability.

"Life isn't short, it's actually very long. The sense of brevity has to do with the fact that most days are the copy of a copy. Since there is no surprise, logically there is a temporary entrapment. It is felt in an eternal present, until a change happens. That's when you realize you've lost something, and it all happened so fast.

What I am saying is that, just as a normal individual sees it in his work, a romantic, melancholy, depressed, apathetic individual may feel this in his life. A no change, an anchorage in the present, always the same and suffocating. Desiring change this way, by hook or by crook."

"Who, before going to work, wouldn't push a fast rewind button? So, when you hit play, when you really wanted to live, it would be at the end of the day. How many wouldn't rewind many days, months, years, or even life itself...?

Life is not good or bad, it is not a blessed gift, it is not important or magical. It's boring, apathetic, meaningless, and subject to forces, in which most of the time, you can only be the spectator.

There will be those who make a living, doing what they like; it's like living twice! They don't have to disconnect mind and heart. There are *those who will live adventures, and will be surprised to meet different people.... Although in 30 years, I have only seen it in books and movies.*

Whoever says that life is there, and that it is necessary to make an effort to live it to the full, and to be happy, should put those words where those words fit. They are sapphire individuals, who believe that just blowing a flute, they will hear a fabulous melody. Perhaps that painful and annoying sound is enough for them. But to an idealist, someone who knows exactly what he wants to buy in a store, and doesn't want anything else, someone who is designed, despite himself, to listen to a fluid melody, will find it stupid to play the flute, if he doesn't know. In addition, you must have the necessary resources to get your hands on the flute...

If you don't like something, you don't like it, period. To struggle, to fight to get you to like something, is useless. It doesn't matter if you kick, cry or get angry, but the reality is that we don't choose what we like. Tastes can change, but by themselves, as a natural process.

No matter how hard I try, I don't think I'm going to get to like fish, kiwifruit, the damn Care Bears, or men sexually speaking. I know what I like, we all know, even if they are sweet and salty things at the same time, things that are in opposition, or even if they are bitter things.

If you add the work, the time you spend sleeping, the free time you spend in boring routine, and the surprises or changes that are bad, what you have left is rather little of true fulfillment. Everything else can quietly go to oblivion, to death, as if it never happened."

*Basically, **life is short when positive stimuli are scarce. The more stimulus, the more you live**. Each person will be stimulated in a different way, and the truth is that normally, we cannot choose either what stimulates us or the source of stimulation that should provide us with those stimuli.*

THE SOUL ROTS TOO.

"Thus, what is supposed to be the essence of our being is also subject to variation. Either by accident, by the simple passage of time, or by the lack of stimulation. That is perhaps why there is such apathy, such lack of curiosity, such general changes that lead to maturity.

When you look in the mirror, you don't just have to realize your superficial change. You should also be aware of your visceral and skeletal change and, logically, of the neuronal substrate that your identity involves.

When it comes to <u>stimulation</u>, it's as if every single thing that attracts us is like a vessel. And these glasses, little by little, fill up. Once they are filled, they are no longer used. Although you feel more and more full of experiences, paradoxically, you feel emptier, as if you are missing something, as if you have lost that part you have filled forever.

I imagine the ideal would be to act like the dogs, who always go after the ball because they always find it funny. But of course, I suppose that this would not be very adaptive for us.

There are things you do so many times, that you don't need to do; you just need to imagine those things, and it produces the same result. That is to say, the soul also rots, producing that categorical emptying. That's growing up."

<u>**MAN IS THE ONLY ANIMAL THAT HAS A HOLE IN ITS HEART**</u>.

Why then, does the human being tend to want to hoard and accumulate all kinds of useless or expendable things? He not only accumulates these things, but also invests a great deal of resources, and in some cases, his entire life.

The things he tries to fill that bottomless hole in his heart with are very varied. Things such as: unused property, empty relationships, useless devices that save you time (just so you can spend it on other unhealthy activities), fighting fiercely to bankrupt a few hundred families, just to have another zero in his bank account....etc.

The animals, they hunt and gather what they need. Because they know that the most important thing in life is to live.

It's true that you have to plan, and you have to cover your ass. But at a certain point of security, you can't ask life for more, you can't ask it to behave in this or that way. Animals live the present in their minds, they do not have the powerful projective capacity of human beings.

Human beings..., we see our own death. This is the hole, this is what frightens us, what we want to forget, or we try to cover it up. The people who engage in these behaviors (who are almost all of them in our society), in my view, reflect great insecurity, and the need to narcotize the idea that one day they will have an end. To me, they are no different than drunks, or addicts to any kind of thing...

__I do not propose that we should return to the animal kingdom, and behave as such, but I do say that it is necessary to live to live, to fight for what your life really is, to put aside all those layers, which only make you forget and cover what is inside.__

Those who carry out these narcotic activities existentially, and know this, do not want to redirect their animal aggressiveness, because they enjoy damaging and hoarding. These people would be what our society defines as evil, and instead, are seen as respectable people. It operates in them the camouflage of hypocrisy, and of the funnel-shaped social system that they provide to their vassals; they generate for them the illusion that one day they too can become King. So, everyone is happy and everything is in place. The age of marketing.

I frankly don't give a damn. For me, it is their right, because they are the predators of the social ecosystem, another species. You can't ask the lion not to eat lamb, or the other way around. But you have to be very naive, or want to be like them, to admire them. They are different, nothing more; as symbolic animals, their food is the suffering of others. Either you develop skills so you don't get caught, or they devour you when they have the right. It is normal, within our species are those who would enjoy living alone, and those who need the life of others to enjoy it.

From the point of view of <u>animal learning and conditioning</u>, I seem to be supported by the concept of **learned helplessness**. Based on this, on the subject's lack of control over the reinforcing consequences.

When the consequences are independent of the behavior, a state of learned helplessness develops. This is manifested in a lack of motivation, reflected in a decrease in execution and greater passivity. It also gives rise to a widespread expectation that the behaviour will remain independent of the reinforcing consequences. Defencelessness manifests itself not only through a deficit in learning, but also through the fact of learning that...

<u>**...CONDUCT AND REWARD ARE INDEPENDENT...**</u>

You acquire a greater ability to see what doesn't add up. I mean, you mature faster.

You understand the house of cards that is life itself, when you see the randomness that underlies every dance of variables. When you see everything as more aseptic and objective, you change. ***The attractiveness of a promise, of something better, or something you intuit unstable, is lost.***

When you think you control, when your ego is identified and strong, you tend to see less of everything that is not controllable. You see less dependence on variables, even when you intuit them. In this way, you continue to take for granted many things, which at any given moment do not have to be so, because everything has changed. You think everything is more stable, because you're still focused on your goal. With the unlikely hope, but anticipated enjoyment.

The most important thing for someone who has faith is to keep it. He will defend it at all costs, because he knows that without it, his whole ego will collapse.

When you see better the dependence on things, and you change, you mature, you rot..., but in return, you are more lethal to adaptation, even if you are isolated. Faith is for the flock.

The one who survives loneliness and despair must logically have more weapons and skills.

CRASHED OR BORN WITH STAR.

There are people, no matter what they do, they're going to play it right. Others, on the other hand, no matter how hard they try and put in the effort, they will not avoid the debacle.

Put that way, it seems like a cheap excuse for a crybaby. Flipping a coin, I've been flipped up to eight times in a row. A 50% chance of occurrence event. Normally you have to throw it away many times to get rid of this pattern, but in the long run, it happens.

That is to say, if we suppose that in the life of an individual there are 8 specific moments dependent on chance, in which life would have changed radically if something else had happened, we can assure that there will be people whose result is always positive, and others always negative. Normally, of course, a person will get one of lime and one of sand. These types of people are the most abundant. The rest of the people, extremes, will represent a small percentage.

With this simple reflection, it seems more credible, the idea that there are people who always have the black one, or that a gray cloud raining down on them perpetually accompanies them.

Another curious reading is the fact that these people of the central part, and those who have good luck stars, will attribute all the merit of their successes to the formidable will of their ego. They will tend to mess with the crashed ones, to tell them that it is possible to change their luck with effort, and if they are this way, it is because they deserve it. In life, there are fortunate, gracious people, people who come out of trouble easily, and others who attract trouble. Appraisals such as this one are another blow to our supposedly very powerful "I".

HOW TO WIN IN THE LONG TERM.

In life decision making, as long as they are not all-or-nothing situations, where you have to choose and act without prior evaluation; or in situations where you have to risk everything because you have no other choice even with little chance of success, the way to win is always the following in the long term:

In order not to be fooled by the carrot that hangs in front of you, you have to be free from all influence, and first of all, know what success means to you.

For one, success can be a doctor, a teacher, a housewife. Or, like in the "Leaving Las Vegas" movie, drinking yourself to death. As much as our society wants to impose a single model on us, the truth is that there are as many models of success as there are goals in the twisted mind of the human being. It can be applied not only to goals that encompass a lifetime, but also to small goals.

Once you have a clear view of your goal, continuing to be drawn from prejudices and social influences, what you need to do is to assess the value of the goal as objectively as possible. Weigh what you have to pay to get it, and most importantly, the probability of getting it.

You have to think objectively, about the best that can happen to you, about the worst, and think about what would be halfway through. Now, split in half again, from the worst to the first partition, and bet on it.

This would be like betting 0.25 cents, to win 1 euro, with a 50% chance of success, in the long term you always win. If you bet on the first partition, you'll always be the same. In this case, it would be like betting 0.5 cents to get 1 euro with the probability of 50%. As entertainment all right, but in the long term you earn nothing. If you bet beyond this first partition, you are betting on **hope and faith, unlikely**. And if the situation repeats too much, you're going to lose irretrievably. It would be like betting 0.75 cents, for 1 euro, at 50%. If you bet on the worst, you'll be **pessimistic, and you'll be losing your chances of winning**. It's the fact that you don't bet anything, that you close yourself off from possible opportunities for success.

It doesn't have to be dishonorable or unworthy, like a failure, to abandon a dream. To be brave is to have the strength to try to achieve the goal, not the fact of achieving it. Besides, the only one who should care about that is yourself. If it seems to you that you've done what you could, and that your conscience won't bother you: "Let me go warm, let the people laugh."

A dream must be like a star that guides a ship in the deepest night:
 To steer a course, and not be stumbling around, that's fine. But if this dream leads you to crush the ship against treacherous reefs, get you directly into a fatal storm, or exhaust your men with hunger and thirst, it is better to abandon that ungrateful star and follow another. Or, instead, you can simply explore, or be there... If you want to be shipwrecked on purpose, or for honor, because you owe it to someone or yourself, it's better to turn around and blow up the boat somewhere else. The star that tortured you, let her go to hell!

So far, I've messed with society. The next level, which encompasses this one, is that of life, as a component unrelated to death. I mess with the vision of life that most people have of life: that life is a ray of light, that it illuminates the darkness of the universe, as if we were the center, and it was made for us.

LIFE IS ONLY REFINED DEATH.

We ourselves have put on the label of humans, as if we were on a very different and privileged plane of the animal kingdom. We ourselves, who have separated from the idea of death, from inert matter. In reality, life is a different form of death.

If matter is the daughter of nothing, and we are the children of matter, somehow we are the children of nothing. At least we're closely related to her.

From a cherry tree, cherries come out. From a wolf, wolves come out. Out of nowhere, death and life come out.

It is true that there is an evolution, but what I am referring to, is that even though we are another component element, on the whole,;we are not so different from the root from which we came out. Life originated from an association and recombination at the subatomic level, as a result of variations contributed by energy in the carbon molecule.

We all need energy, to keep stable, not only our physical structures, but also our mental ones.

Pregnant women do not create their children by themselves, but by the orders of genetic engineering. And even if the child comes out of his flesh, that flesh must be sustained by things that come out of the Earth.

She feeds on plants, on animals; they also feed on the ground. The Earth, the inert matter. All living beings, we are formed by something lifeless: water. This one, in its evolution, has been able to belong to so many beings and places, that it would be impossible to follow its path.

That is, we come out of the Earth, we sustain ourselves from the Earth, and when our end comes, we return to the Earth. An element so dependent on the earth, by force, must be made up of earth. We are soil that walks and thinks, that's all.

In our society, death is a subject of little use. We are made to believe that there is still time, that we have control over when, and how, we are going to die. The truth is, though, that death respects no one and nothing.

If you look at the small print of the contract signed with her, it clearly states: "You belong to me, I will come for you whenever I want. Make no mistake, I won't give you anything, I'll lend it to you."

I suppose that is not the case in other societies. We visit death every time we sleep, every time we forget something slowly, every time we feed on it, every time we choose one option, discarding the other.

I think, the first thing a person should understand, is that one day he's going to die.

Only from this perspective can you live a more fulfilling life. **When you are aware that one day you are going to give up everything, things are seen in their true magnitude.** Thus, many of the little things we care about would normally no longer make sense. Knowing that each moment is unique and unrepeatable gives you the ability to do those things you want and you like, not those that others want. You only live one life, and it is very sad to live it from suffering, acceptance, pain.

Thus, there should be no fear in knowing what you want, and rebelling against the rest. For no one can take something from you that will be taken away, eventually, by time. Deep down, there's nothing to lose, because whatever you do, nothing endures. It's only a matter of time before everything is founded on the oblivion of the universe.

There should be no fear of life, no fear of death, no fear of what they might do to you in the meantime, because absolutely everything is borrowed. Even if they take something from you along the way, in the end, time will take everything from you, and it will be as if you never existed.

It will be, as if the world had been a dream for you, as if the world were just a place where dreams meet, being all that only... a dream.

Some naive person will say that this is the reason for having children, and for doing great deeds that will leave your mark on history. But that's like peeing in a creek, and saying your urine will last. If the water is crystal clear, you can still proudly track it down three feet. But if you keep looking beyond, you'll soon see it fade into the water. Some waters, which will end up in the sea; such an immensity, that it is stupid to think, being sane, where that little representation of your being will end up. We belong to the whole, we are the whole, and the one who is perpetuated is the whole. If not, from where did you get the water so you could pee on it?

When you look to the horizon and see how the gaseous mass that makes up the sky is confused with the Earth and seems to have the same texture, it is as if it were made of the same material. It becomes inevitable to compare the sky with plants and people. As if it were a painting, you see the people melting in the distance, with the horizon and the landscape, looking the same texture. They look like they're made of the same material, but with movement. A movement similar to billiard balls.

<u>The initial opening in the billiard table</u> has apparently free trajectories, but in reality, they are already determined by the angle and strength of the stroke. A skilled player calculates the hit, the angle, the bounce. If there were a supercomputer, which would allow us to calculate even the smallest of the variables that make up our life, we could see our future. I mean, it could see our destiny, already determined.

Whether it is all life or all death, it is clear to me that all this volubility and precariousness cannot be differentiated by simply putting a label or a name, because from an integrating point of view, everything is the same.

Leaving behind the subsystems of life and death, the next step is to mess with the universe as a whole. The last great blow that I suffered, I got it thanks to a co-worker, whose **psychological firewall** was that of a staunch Christian. It was the total fall of the power of reason:

The firewall lets in only those stimuli that are enabled, blocking the rest. Let's say, it offers a certain parcel of the reality.

Thus, for a <u>normal individual</u>, that with which he interacts psychologically will be only that which is adaptive. He will use only instrumental information. He'll be pragmatic about his life.

For an <u>unbalanced individual</u>, there would be pathways through which unwanted mental elements would enter.

<u>Someone looking for the whole truth</u>..., it's like being naked, without any kind of firewall.

This program shows the total reality, or parcels of it. What lets you see the boundaries is your subjectivity. The funny thing is, that entity that restricts and controls entry, is also real.

Returning to the subject of the servant of the Lord....

My reasons could not break her faith, a faith based precisely on that, on believing without asking questions. You can't reason with someone who uses different communication channels. It made me doubt everything; not by believing in a god, but by realizing that he was real, since he was real to her. This is so, because this concept is what drove her to live her life in a happy and transcendental way. <u>The lie is real, and it can be very adaptive</u>.

You live what you perceive, as if it were your particular dream. That which you do not

perceive, that which happens outside your life or knowledge, is as if it did not exist.

DREAMS, REALITIES, LOGIC IS ONLY PART OF THE DREAM.

Is a linear and eternal universe like that of Christians possible? Is the form of the universe like that? Is there parallel universes? Is our version of reality so firm, when there are regions of the universe where the basic laws of physics do not even apply? How is it possible that when I was a child, dreaming, I saw places in a village where I had never been before? What is the explanation for that, even in my dreams, I connected with my brothers hundreds of kilometres away, and attended the moment when he found a package of toys lying in the ground, in the same order of collection?

All this has led me to question Reason with great frustration.

It is possible that it is only an archaic tool, with which the organism adapts to survive. It seems most appropriate to think that the mind serves the body, to help it to exist and to reproduce.

The wind can move you, and cause you to fall, even if you don't see it or know where it comes from. An idea or voice can also cause you to fall, and therefore it is real.

The different voices or perspectives, whether in an integrated way or disorderly as a result of mental illness, are also real.

So, a dead writer, who transmits his ideas, is real. Thus, the whole culture, as a constantly evolving entity, is real; the god of the Christian, or the Muslim, is also real; any belief is real!

There are so many realities, that they transcend the concept of reality. Each of these realities behave as interdependent subsystems, connected to each other, and connected in turn, to an ultimate reality, which we call the universe, God, eternal or not, linear or not, infinite and parallel... It is in all these forms, and none of them.

Our reason cannot trap, embrace, define this concept, because it is like wanting to catch water with a sieve.

The universe is like a big dream with different dreams, interrelated or not. The universe, like a dream, is irrational.

It is by definition irrational, since reason is inside, forming part of that dream. Trying to put the chains of reason on him seems like a pretty childish attempt.

It's easy to understand how each one of us felt that we lived in our world. What does it matter what happens in China? The impact on your routine is negligible. We live, more than in our world, in our dream.

Some may say that the difference between a dream and reality is very clear. He will argue that in reality there are physical laws, temporal coherence, or stable behavior of the variables that make up life. I'm not saying no. But in relation to the whole, this is not what matters most.

This little bubble of rational reality, which makes up our world, is so ridiculous in comparison to all the irrational things in the universe, that you might think that our world is its dream.

Thus, our dreams would be the total reality. Crazy people would see it as it is, without the firewall of reason. Isn't it all a dream, rational or irrational?

The world of the living people, it's just a reflection, a dream of the world of the dead. Are we, our "selves" present, not the result of our dead "selves"?

Purpose of a dream: The purpose of a dream is to dream. A dream has no purpose. The purpose of the moth, to serve the bat. The bat serves the ecosystem. The ecosystem serves the planet. The planet to the universe. The purpose of a dream is to serve all subsystems. It's the link to all dreams. We dream for the universe, and the universe dreams for us.

However, in the end, this does not solve anything for the one who does not have an inertia in his "I". After so much discussion and understanding, for those who have no fear, hope, or responsibility, it comes down to this:

If you like your dream, if you can do something to change it in case you don't like it, how much fatigue will you endure?

Sleeping a deep sleep is pleasant and refreshing, but if in your REM phase the same dull, meaningless litany is repeated over and over again...

—<u>Lack of vital inertia phase</u>.

It would not be a phase of depression or inactivity. I am referring more to the fact of withdrawing into oneself, of returning to the root or essence of one's being, when everything has fallen around you; like the cat that struggles on its belly. I'm talking about getting your quiet, apart from the world.

<u>ALL OF THE ABOVE IS USELESS</u>.

It may be a definition of a person's state of being, and of the configuration of the universe, but... the only reality is that I have always had no appetite for almost everything that ordinary people enjoy. I have tried to seek pleasures, and to have faith, in vain things for myself.

It can be improved in one aspect, or competitive system, but, hell, there is no better human being than another.

Nothing's right, anything works. I don't like anything, I've always been bored of everything. Since I was 7 months old I was not looking for freedom, but curiosity to see if there was something more entertaining outside the crib. I'm a bland man.

And I can never get better, adapt. Because, what the fuck, you can't improve on making something interesting, playful, pleasant, or attractive for you.

What I propose is that if everything that was there really has failed you, you do not share the idea of success, and you have not achieved that any pleasure or vice seduces you, the best thing would be to make your own camp in the abyss of your being.

It would be like looking for an isolated house, and surrounding it with barriers, traps and visible and audible signs of not passing, danger. This way, you would only have to sit in the entrance of your house, quiet and safe, that the first one to show his face, would do so with the sole intention of annoying you.

Then, as the intruder jumped over the barrier of fire and thorns, you would have every right and pleasure to shoot him in the chest with a shotgun.

If someone really wants something good, or to get to know you, they won't get into it; they'll listen to the signs at the entrance. It will be communicated in advance via telephone, e-mail, letter, or smoke signals.

It doesn't necessarily have to be physical isolation, of course. It's the fact of being in your place, and saying openly, that you're no longer for jokes, or putting up with air salesmen.

There is nothing to gain or lose, and you owe nothing to the idea of cooperation. The barriers that would define, or limit your parcel, would be some simple guidelines that would be defined by my current idea of the...

... honor: To do good to what is good for you, and evil to what is bad for you. In both cases, if possible, by far.

That's how you define which side you play on, which is your shirt. If you are one of the bad guys, or the ones who pass everything over, it is because nobody has done anything good for you and you owe nothing to the supposed good.

If you're one of the good guys, it's because someone has helped you, and you have to give it back to them; or because you know, in other circumstances, that person, entity or whatever, would do the same for you.

If (whatever it is: God, or life itself for example), they don't care about you, then you don't listen to them either...

It seems simple, but in reality it is. If Bin Laden himself saves my ass, no matter what happens in the world, and if it doesn't conflict with other ideas of mine, I will owe him the favor, positioning myself against the world. I will not defend what has spit on me, and bite the hand of the one who has fed me!

Besides, heroes and villains, there are on all sides. The villain of one side is the hero of the other. Everyone will have to defend what they belong to.

The reading that can basically be made of this, on a general level, is that if in the human being, people help each other more than they attack, in the end everyone will really help and cooperate. And if there is more aggression than mutual aid, then let it all go to hell, it doesn't matter.

Another concept, closely linked to that of the armoured house, is that of the garden: it would be the small or large things that we like, but in any case, that we control. It can be having tea, playing an instrument, walking, watching movies, cooking, real relationships....etc. All these things would be the ***flowers in the garden***.

Tastes, I think, are the most basic element, which is already there, and although they may change, they are known for sure. Either you like something, or you don't like it, or you don't care. What you don't know if you like it or not is that you don't really care. There may be conflict of taste and having to choose, but if you could choose both, you would choose both.

The needs are within the tastes. The individual, even in a state of madness, is able to discern what he likes or dislikes, just like a small child at birth, or even plants. That natural affinity for something is the most basic orientation.

Our society of enjoyment, or well-being, is therefore very basic to the few alternatives of those who have existential tastes, or who need a different purpose in life. Nowadays, great intellectual coefficients are preferred, with little projective or spiritual intelligence; the latter is necessary to give meaning to life higher (not better) than oneself. In other words, robots are now required to serve society.

In short, for me, the garden would be made up of those little tastes that can be enjoyed every day, that are more or less stable, and if possible, that do not harm you too much. It is also possible to have existential tastes, but which depend solely and exclusively on you, or on what you can control. In my case, I suppose it would be the idea that everything is dreamy, like a movie. Everything is perception.

I think wildflowers are overrated. If you find them, enjoy them, but it's not worth neglecting your garden looking for others...

I speak of **_being a sleeper_**, of being an open, ambiguous person, given to help, or to the most ruthless aggression. Depending on the element that enters your garden. This would be done after a previous evaluation of whether you can do it without having to sacrifice house, garden, and the divine verb. It's the waiting on the porch, seeing what's going on in the world, and how it's going to affect you as you enjoy your garden.

It is a feeling, that exists between anger and calm. It does not mean apathy or depression. It is the fact of enjoying what is truly yours, but being for the world a latent element. It is indifference to that which is not you, or has not brought you anything. Waiting for action.

Without surprise, without anything that attracts your curiosity or attention, without pleasure in what is your real life, is it not better to sleep?

If your life doesn't offer you anything, don't pay attention to it, detach it, look at it as what it is: an absurd and meaningless routine. Sleep until something interests you, or until the end.

That way you win for sure, no one can stop you from sleeping, no death, no nothing, no monkey crazy about his social system.

Action-reaction, and enjoy your garden, your treasure, until it also merges with the whole from which it came.

Sleeping is like hearing the melody of life, but very far away and distant. For those who find it hurtful to pay attention to something that does not stimulate, attract, or entertain them, it is better to lower the volume of that dream that is their life. And if something interesting happens that catches your eye, you can go back online. We all like to sleep in bed, and rest.

Evaluate whether the pain you get from fruitless searching is preferable to pleasure, in net terms. Observe, when you are absent, how the changes that take place without being forced, take you to your destination. If you're not made to enjoy, you won't be able to enjoy. Do not be so arrogant as to think that your almighty will can change even your most basic nature.

It's like being blind from birth, and wanting to see with your ass. You can try to see, or you can pretend to see with your ass. You can imitate the gestures of normal people. Even getting to believe yourself that you see.

But deep down you don't see shit, you're not comfortable, you don't understand what it's like to see.

You can endure some time by pretending or believing you see; some will hang on for life. But if you don't have a reason, like a duty, a theatrical actor's vocation, or some pleasure that overcomes pain, the best thing is to take your ass and put it with your kind, with the blind people.

It's better not to force what you don't really have control over. Let that which you do not master flow. Because deep down, it doesn't belong to you, otherwise you'd control it like you control your hand.

You have to accept that in the end, absolutely everything you borrow has to be paid back.

<u>When should we let it flow, give it back?</u> When you realize that the end of this thing has come, this goal, this relationship, this life... You know that you have to give it back when it gets out of hand. <u>When you realize you're not handling that element. When the system drives you around, and gives you nothing in return.</u>

Sleeping is nice. It is a way of enjoying life, from the denial of it, for those who do not like it too much. Thus avoiding the precipitous transit, until you feel it is completely necessary.

When you are straddling between the living, the dead, and the to be, no vital act will make you feel fully alive. Curiously, no self-destructive or destructive act will make you feel dead. Simply because you exist outside yourself, as part of the whole, floating between your body or the hereafter, waiting for something to tip the scales. You're in limbo, asleep.

With everything that's been said since the beginning of the book:
 I have provided a rational and irrational explanation. I have provided some pleasures and motivations. I have provided a behavioral hierarchy, and I have provided some purposes or goals.

ORIENTAL THINKING AND MY POSITION.

In oriental cultures, the concept of intelligence has other more spiritual and practical features, when it comes to living life to the fullest, looking it in the face, without too many artifices.

I'm probably more inclined towards this kind of ability, maybe that's why I've been attracted to the Oriental world. ***Occidental psychology only seems to study how our mind works, but not what it is used for from an existential point of view***, which after all, is what matters to give meaning to your life.

You can understand how an engine works, fix it, and get it ready for the journey. But if you don't know where you're going, or where you should, or want to, you can spend your time in any other stupid way. I believe that today, many people at the individual level, and society at the general level, would need more than health, money and love: direction.

The Oriental thought (Buddhism, Hinduism...), proposes a cooperative and candid individual. It is a preliminary step towards enlightenment, for all beings deserve respect and harmony as a whole.

I propose a system more like an ecosystem of the animal kingdom (which is what really exists), in which everyone interacts with his or her truth, or dream, to achieve calm. The nature of each one is already given automatically. I propose a release.

If we all help, we all owe each other something, and humanity will work together. But if a greater percentage of people attack, whether for pleasure or necessity, humanity will tend to eliminate themselves and that is how it should be. If the two things alternate, the equation will still be unresolved. How it ends, it doesn't matter. There is no high purpose, although it is true that we could do better with a little common sense.

It's not so terrible to be alone, and do things on your own. It has the great advantage that you only have to worry about your skin.

Let the matter solve itself. Let each one know where belongs, what has nourished and given him light to grow. In the end, it'll all be over or dreamed of again..., who cares!

All the elements of the universe have that something in common:
 Energy interdependence between systems, more like dreams than physical realities. But to ask that everything be harmonized without harm, without energetic change, is naive.

In fact, everything is already harmonized, from the first cell that began to devour other cells as a way of obtaining energy, and it went better. To harmonize it in our own way, making us all part of the same being, would be nice. But today, we only have the potential; scarce, but we have it.

It seems that it was yesterday, when we came down from the trees. That's the way it is, even if you want to look the other way.

We have to accept the evolutionary point we are at. This is what I mean by liberation. It is the liberation from all lies and predispositions, from a society in which all tell themselves, little less than that they are God, and that they are free from all evil. Everybody says it to each other, and they believe it. Whatever happens, you have to smile, as if you had just been told a joke. Everybody's happy, pretending to be happy.

Well, the system's been great. Saying that you're tired, and that there are certain things you're not going to put up with, puts you in the spotlight. They stigmatize you.

They say you're sick, and they'll try to take you back to the world of **congratulatory zombies**. When all you want is to be calm. Everyone's hyperactivated, doing hyperbullshits.

We are not animals, nor are we gods; **we are super monkeys**. From my point of view, we should start acting like it.

To be in harmony, for some people, is to be against others.

I propose that the individual exists floating in the whole collectivity. And that when he acts, (as when the clutch is engaged to the engine), he does so by taking part in the role he has to play, the dream he has to live, without feeling overwhelmed.

The oriental culture, proposes an individual existing in the present of the here and now, within itself. In addition, it aims to orient its actions towards a harmonious, twinned and even virtuous collective whole. Actually, the whole dream isn't like that.

It seems that the direction is reversed. But somehow, in this point of view of mine, it seems to me that I have joined the strength, the activation of Occidental thought, and the calm, spiritual serenity, of the Orient. All this is integrated through respect and understanding. Also, in an automatic, involuntary way. Thus connecting us to the rest of the elements of the universe, and to God.

I suppose what I have done is to try to analyze how to manage these two aspects of action and peace.
 If something attacks you, you have the option of fighting, running away....
 If you are calm, learn to continue being calm, bringing more serenity.

It makes little sense to get into the lotus posture when you're surrounded by wolves. And it doesn't make much sense to beat up someone who's helpless and hasn't done anything to you.

Any one of these vital approaches, in its harshest or dogmatic version, sounds like a mass scam.

Occidental culture, confronted the vision of death with the development of a pragmatic, aggressive, individualistic logic.

The Oriental culture, from the supposed pessimism, apathy, faced it by listening to it directly without artifices.

Some of them developed a great activity, through a deification of the "I". The others were paralyzed, diluted within themselves.

I believe in a very small self, like a whisper, a dream that disappears at times, but with a high

power of activation. Between anger and calm. Between the waiting and the fierce, almost suicidal fight. At the point where the beginning and the end meet, in eternity. In the irrationality of a dream, which you don't know if you live, but you do know what you perceive.

To dream or not to dream is the only question. Everything else...

—<u>Internal aggression.</u>

I have decided to refer to this concept at the end. Because with the fall of that which influenced you, the channels or pathways that were activated also fall into disuse. These pathways would be receptors inside you.

The fact that you have a loaded and ready shotgun, plus an unbearable boredom that invades you despite being in your garden, can lead you to want to practice on your property, on yourself.

"Loneliness is feeling locked up inside yourself. The self-destructive behaviors would be like being in that cell of loneliness, and having a guy next to you that you don't like, that torments you. Turns out that this guy is you. Getting along with him is the key.

Some people get on badly with themselves only temporarily, this would be logical, and adaptive. After another identity is generated, the previous one must be pruned. Others will get along badly with him forever, and when they want to kill him, they know that they are also killing themselves."

Anyway, the usual, that in spite of all the planning, you get so bored that it hurts to endure all that boredom. The inertia of having destroyed everything around you, and seeing that nothing is stable, can lead you to continue in this maelstrom of destruction. Of course, all that's left now is you on the horizon, your house and your garden. It is pleasant, in this way, to slowly self-destruct yourself. Hitting rock bottom is like getting to the top of a hit, only by changing the perspective. For rabid, unhappy and dilute people it can be very attractive. Wanting to end the source of your pain and misery by blaming it on you.

And the most serious, causing you a pleasure, and a sense of control, difficult to describe. You squeeze your own neck, telling yourself you're the boss. You let yourself go, to revive, and to catch yourself again. You enjoy being a bully. How do you try to avoid it, or at least recognize yourself as one of these people without doing too much damage?

We'll all die, and nothing makes any sense. Without values, without direction, without pleasures that consume you, the only question that remains is:

<u>**WOULD YOU RATHER DIE LIKE A DOG, OR LIKE A HUMAN BEING?**</u>

That is, wandering around like a dog lost in the rain, trying to enjoy things that also bore you, or respecting yourself, stopping hating you, waiting for the end, but fighting against what you think is attacking you externally; whether it's other people, God, or life itself; whatever you are not yourself.

It is like an aesthetic towards yourself, even though you are in the deepest depths of the abyss, in the deepest solitude.

If you walk around in the shadows, among the ***predators of the abyss***, you will only find broken people.

They're aimless, totally lost, self-destructive people. Maybe waiting for someone to fix them. They are people who do not have a base camp in the abyss, who do not have a home. They have no garden to defend, so they wander, sometimes preying, sometimes being preyed upon.

They are with you in the abyss, but either because they do not have a rich inner world, or because they do not know, or cannot manage their pain, they are different from the one who faces the survival of an existential void, taking refuge within himself.

These others (the dwellers of the abyss) like to relate to each other. They see as normal the absence of a minimum of reciprocity. They are even more hypocritical, selfish and competitive than in the original base camp.

At least you can see them coming...

They come to tell you straight up that they're going to play poker with you, cheat on you, and leave you naked. After you've been plucked, they'll slap you twice on the back and say, "It's okay, kid, that's life. Today I'll pluck you, tomorrow you'll pluck me, it doesn't matter."

I believe that among these people there is no true companionship, because **to love another person, whatever it may be, it is a necessary condition to be someone**; to be materialized in this reality, **to love yourself**.

There will be some momentarily lost, because they have just fallen into the abyss. Others will be at the wellhead, trying to climb back up again. God knows, how many times they've tried...

There are those who have given up. Those who accept, that the camp is not for them. Among those who already have a sore ass after so many falls, there will be some looking for a place to make a home. These are the ones who understand that only those who really belong to that world can permanently ascend. They stop stubbornly and stop listening to those who demand it from above. The campers don't realize that this kind of people suffocate there. They're like fish out of water.

But most of them, when they hit the ground, they broke. They wander around, just like that, maybe hoping to find someone to fix them. They are fragmented beings. This huge well, which forms the rest of the camp, is like a human garbage dump. Like a junkyard, where you can buy the parts, but not the whole vehicle. They may be functional, at different levels of your life, but your vision of life is impaired.

These places are like centers of slow suicide, as well as the routine of an anodyne life, on the surface.

The campers would have this altered, undamaged vision. His hallucinogenic and syrupy perspective would be determined by lies, hypocrisy and pettiness.

The ones on the outside, shaped by the truth. The ones on the inside, shaped by the lie.

With dying like a dog, I'm not saying that dogs, for example, are short, dirty. But I think a human being might have a behavior of his own. Not higher, or necessarily complex, but pending its symbolic world.

Perhaps we are what we are meant to be, and humanity as a whole has already reached its potential. Everything fights, we all fight....

But fighting against yourself, if not by disease or as a phase, is a much worse feeling than the pain of fighting against other people. It's a worse feeling than fighting for nothing. It's not just empty, it's guilt. With the tension of getting rid of yourself once and for all, or pulling away, putting up with the traps you set yourself, to fall, just for fun. There are no adventures, just empty, meaningless tricks that take up your time.

It takes a lot of strength to be able to fight with yourself, to destroy yourself, either slowly or suddenly. These people are not afraid of anything except pain. But it's always better to take it out, not put it in deeper, whining.

The flag down: If you're surrounded by enemies, and you know the goal, the flag, is down. If you know there will be no victory, no glory, no transcendence. If you only see beings, who seem made to kill each other, with any kind of excuse:

Is it better to lie on the ground, curl up, and let yourself be killed indolently? Get drunk, and wait for them to give you transit to the afterlife?

Being annoyed, yes or no, if you don't feel sorry for yourself, the first 2 options in front of the fallen flag are very valid. But if you imagine yourself in that situation and feel sorry for yourself, that means that with the third option you can gain something: respect for yourself, and respect from the" whole".

You will gain that little satisfaction, the little pride, the gesture of appreciation for yourself.

If nothing or no one appreciates you, or respects you, do it yourself. Or at least don't join them... Respect and appreciate yourself. That way, you will die knowing that at least someone has loved you, even if you are yourself. Even if you have no high purpose, no hopes, no duties, no fears. If only to keep your body and mind, waiting for something worthwhile, or the arrival of death.

Thus, what was the problem, the psychosis generated by the different "I's", is also the solution to the problem:

The idea is that the executive, apart from giving the information, should not allow any voice to act separately. It must distance itself so much from the core of your "I", which will exercise protection in the distance, as a *guardian*.

Being fragmented, goals are obtained but from each voice, separately. For these, the voices as a whole do not come to say anything that translates the operating memory. All they hear is noise. We remain, in essence, just that translation of information.

What we can do is to generate a central "I", as an executive, a guardian, who will have one goal: to protect the system.

This guardian, being far away, will not hear the noise, and consequently will be able to firmly comply with this single, nonpropositive command. That his function is not to destroy, waiting, is very important. In this way, it can act even when the volitional system falls, as it is not part of it.

I believe that, deep down, normal and adapted people work that way, formed by that innate selfishness that pulls in one direction, without making noise to them.

In a broken individual, the voices alternated in total control, won by vote, so to speak. But when it came to taking action, they did it themselves, following a whole or nothing, with the subsequent consequences that this entails. It is necessary, an integration of all of them, informative, and a sovereign executive who takes action under that simple rule.

I had not found this guardian or executive self, because without goals, without a consensual order of voices, it is gone, leaving its sovereignty free. Then, its place is taken by other voices, always taking you to the same thing if there is no agreement.

Normally indifference rules, since there is no goal; let's say you deal with the pleasure and the strength of aggression to fuck everything up, even yourself; and with it comes depression. It would be like some kind of mental apoptosis. On the other hand, if you give your guardian this clear order, he will never move from his place. So, even in the most absolute chaos, their priority will be to protect and wait for another clear order. That's how people with a normal ego work.

I think it's possible to make the executive happy and bring him back. You achieve this by making him believe that his aim is to love and protect the different people who make up his being.

It is possible to think, then, that I am rebelling against myself when I say that we have a control. But this one is only a <u>guardian</u>, a rule that will exist naturally in most people. It's automatic. What happens is that, <u>when it is damaged, it is blocked by the large amount of conflicting information. The way to fix it is to distance it, if possible</u>.

How do you know if you don't have an executive, a spokesman, or if you can get him back?

The president enters the room. Possibly, what happens to a person without purposes or goals that do not make sense of anything, is that in that meeting of different people, each time, a different person has been seated in the chair of the president. In this way, different goals and opposing directions were generated, which fragmented the personality, the being, and produced intense pain.

The chairman would be the spokesman, who would give the guardian the outcome of the meeting. <u>The president integrates</u>. Watch out, not the one in charge. The other members are in charge, each with a share.

If the president finds nothing of external interest, and can't leave anyone in charge, nor the indifference that leads to depression, then he should direct the goals toward himself. And logically, <u>if there are no internal goals, he must secure the guardian and nullify this peculiar democracy until there is something clear.</u>

If the group wants nothing, they should at least fight to keep the group. Thus, they will not commit the ignominy of confronting each other, laughing at it, the rest of the companies.

Leaving the guardian in charge of protection is the last gesture the president can make for the company.

If the president is able to laugh with the rest of the companies, or run away, it's okay for the members of the meeting to act without order, adrift, and exposed to any hostility.
 But if the president is in a corner of the chaotic room, looking out the window at the rest of the presidents laughing and going after him. If he feels sorry for the spectacle of inner pain, and his exposure to others. If he has more affection for his people, he must return to his seat and regain executive control.

The fact of defending yourself should be an innate reflection, which should not be repressed, even if there is no direction or goal.

The point is to keep moving forward, without bending your head, as far as the road takes you. Defending that gang of useless people, who don't know how to do anything together, nor agree on the simplest thing, but who individually are lethal.

It is possible, in reality, that the voice of the nobility has reduced their expectations to that one goal. A very subjective definition of good and evil, depending on what is with you or against you, disguised as a president...

If so, this voice of the nobility will be so crushed that it will not try to be God, and will come to fulfill the functions of the spokesman. That is why I have thought of giving it another function, another "I", because it is so different from the previous one

that it could be said to be another. He' is more
mature, wiser. He does not give an address, and
does not propose to give himself up for anything
elevated, he only feels sorry for himself.

Like when you're playing poker, and you bet
everything aggressively, but with intention,
without giving it away. To show on the table, a
little fear or respect, before you go. Hopefully,
you'll give some of them a displeasure. I insist, that
anyone who wants to give the money away should
give it away; it's a matter of taste. But that's not
what a poker player does.

*Being free doesn't mean throwing it all away, even
to yourself. To be free is to take all your integrated
facets, and to walk with or without direction, but
protecting them.*

**—After all, if a person is capable of self-
destruction, he is also capable of self-
protection.—**

Without this last conclusion, a romantic will end
up feeling really bad.
 A normal person takes it for granted. But the
romantic cannot conform, and blames the whole
and himself, wanting to violate them. The romantic
is able to forget himself, perhaps because he has

never found himself. He desperately seeks something better to give himself to, something that fills his feeling that everything is slipping through his fingers.

A nihilist, he's just a romantic who's beaten up, has no strength, is totally disenchanted and disillusioned. Romanticism causes pain, and nihilism, apart from pain, emptiness and disorientation.

I don't know if I can call myself a nihilist, or a romantic, or if I fit in somewhere. But at least, when you read this again, out of boredom, or to laugh for a while at the nonsense that was going through your troubled head, I hope you don't forget that one day I was you, that I was a necessary and previous step, so that you could be who you are now. So don't judge me, and keep in mind, that I'm still somewhere inside you...

No one is special. Surely, others have passed, pass, and will pass, through the same or worse things... Besides, as I said at the beginning, everyone must go through this situation either consciously or not; either during their lifetime, or at the end of it...

Enough whining, and look at your belly button! Heh heh heh.

When I was little, my mother would tell me a fable, or story, that her father told her as a child. It was something like this:

"There was a boy, an old man and a donkey, on the road. The boy was riding on the donkey, and as they passed through a village, people criticized them:

—What a nerve the child who has the poor old man on foot!
So they decided to change.
—Hey —said the old man—, we're going to change, it looks like this is wrong.....

Then when they passed by another town, people were whispering.

—But what a cheeky old rascal to have the poor child on foot! And him, so comfortably mounted on the beast!
The poor old man said:
—Well, let's both try to go on the donkey, and then we'll get it right!

So, it seemed to be going well. But when they passed through the next town, it was the same old thing:

—How cruel they are, to make him carry such a burden, to the poor animal! They'll tear him down!"

Anyway, I didn't imagine as a child that this would hold one of the hardest truths in life:

Some things can't be fixed. Whatever you do, you're screwed. All that remains is to put up with it, and keep going, no matter what they say.

TAKE CARE!

KIND REGARDS

... I...

P. D.: <u>Whatever happens, don't let anything or anyone tell you what you like, only you know it. You just have to listen to yourself.</u>

END

Don Nieve's works on:

Goodreads.

Facebook.

donnieve7@gmail.com